FORDS OF THE SIXTIES

Michael Parris

Foreword by Edsel B. Ford II

California Bill's
Automotive Handbooks

Publishers
Helen V. Fisher
Howard W. Fisher

Editor
Howard W. Fisher

Cover and Interior Design
Gary D. Smith, Performance Design

Cover Photography
Michael Parris

Interior Photography
Michael Parris unless otherwise noted

Copyright © 2004 by Michael Parris

Published by
California Bill's Automotive Handbooks
P.O. Box 91858
Tucson, AZ 85752
520-547-2462

Distributed by
Motorbooks International
729 Prospect Avenue
PO Box 1
Osceola, WI 54020-0001
800-826-6600

ISBN
1-931128-16-2

Printed in China

1 2 3 4 5 6 7 8 9 10 - 07 06 05 04

We would like to thank Ford Motor Company for the use of photos from their collections.

**Library of Congress
Cataloging-in-Publication Data**

Parris, Michael, 1949–
 Fords of the Sixties / Michael Parris;
  foreword by Edsel B. Ford II.
 p. cm.
 Includes index.
 ISBN 1-931128-16-2 (pb.)
 1. Ford automobile–History. I. Title.

 TL215.F7 P38 2004
 629.222'2–dc22   2004043561
                 CIP

Contents

Foreword

How are we to remember an American decade—by a set of footprints left on the moon? My great-grandfather, Henry Ford, suggested a different way of looking at history. Unsatisfied with facts and dates "pressed dead in a book," he believed we could learn more about people, their visions and their aspirations by looking at their material creations. Many of us believe that the cars of the '60s are classic representatives of that decade.

The freedom and mobility of the automobile is a metaphor for the independence of the decade in which the baby boomers came of age. No company was more taken up with expressing that daring, youthful exuberance in our cars than Ford Motor Company.

The decade started with the power and elegance of the Ford Galaxies and Thunderbirds. Who can forget the affordable Falcons and the exciting, all-new Mustang, the car that created its own segment? My father, Henry Ford II, was behind the wheel at Ford throughout the '60s, and no one was more taken up with the combination of styling and performance than he was.

My father brought his passion for auto racing to the fore. Ford led the pack at every racetrack in America and Europe. Stock car racing became even more popular in the '60s with NASCAR-sanctioned events, and Ford was winning on the super speedways with cars like the Talladega. Who can forget Jim Clark's victory at the Indianapolis 500 in a Lotus-Ford? I was at Le Mans in 1966 when the Ford GT40s placed first, second and third in the race which proved that American cars could dominate a European race. Racing brought a great deal of excitement to Ford in the '60s.

So the '60s was a dramatic era, when America's youth and our cars were coming of age together. That excitement is revealed in the Ford cars of the decade, and nowhere is it presented with more insight and enriching detail than in Mike Parris' new book, *Fords of the Sixties*. Mike takes us for a wonderful joyride with Ford through this dynamic decade.

Edsel B. Ford

Car Owner Acknowledgments

Car collectors are a special breed, and the owners listed below helped to make *Fords of the Sixties* come to life. Sharing their time and beautiful vehicles, they gave me the opportunity to photograph the cars and trucks and also to get a feel for the style and power of that era. I would like to give special thanks to Jim and Rick Schmidt and their National Parts Depot Collection, the So-Cal Galaxies Club members and the Windsor, Canada, guys. You will also notice the large number of Michigan cars, all excellent vehicles, with a great team of owners. And thanks to Erin Jessica Lindsay for letting me actually drive her great '63 Cobra. What a nice ride.

Car Owners:

Detroit

Duncan Ford Collection	'60 Falcon, '60 Country Sedan
Steve Farley	'60 Blue Sunliner
Tom Hopkins	'61 Galaxie Starliner
Larry Kalusny	'63 Falcon, '69 F-150
Erin Jessica Lindsay	'63 Cobra CSX 2045
Jim Kunath	'63 Thunderbird
Mike & Jo Hyatt	'64½ Mustang convertible
Nick Holcomb	'65 Mustang Fastback
J. C. Paschal	'66 Mustang Fastback
Bob Hoeksema	'66 GT350 supercharged
Phil Jacobs	'67 Shelby Mustang (competition)
Don & Sandy Olson	'69 F-150
Anthony Lafrate	'69 Mustang Mach I
Vaughn Koshkarian	'69 Torino Talladega

Florida

National Parts Depot Collection—
Jim & Rick Schmidt
'61 Galaxie, '62 Galaxie, '64 Galaxie,
'65 Mustang, '67 Mustang GT,
'68 Shelby GT500KR, '69 Mustang Mach I,
'69 Torino Cobra 428

Windsor, Canada

Dick Robinson	'65 Thunderbird convertible
Vito Campanaro	'67 Shelby GT500, '69 Shelby GT500 convertible
Gary Duffy	'68 Mustang convertible
Dan Ruszczak	'69 Boss 429

California

Dave Harkey	'60 Starliner
Bud & Ellie Meyers	'63 Galaxie 500XL
Brian Lawler	'64 Galaxie 500XL
Michael Jackson	'64 Country Sedan
Tom Howard	'64 Galaxie 500 convertible, '64 Galaxie 500XL
Tom & Agar Yanulaytis	'66 Galaxie 500
Tom & Pam Chronister	'65 Country Sedan, '61 Sunliner, '62 Sunliner
Cliff & Joann Mierczynski	'67 Galaxie 500XL 7-Litre convertible
Carl Kurtz	'67 Galaxie 500 convertible

Thanks to:

- Jim & Rick Schmidt of National Parts Depot for sharing their amazing Ford collection
- Dick Duncan of Duncan Ford for sharing his eclectic collection of Fords and memorabilia
- Rick Titus for great stories of his dad's championship Trans-Am year
- Tom & Pam Chronister and the So-Cal Galaxies Car Club for their all-day photo session

Facts, Figures & Detail Support:

- Ray Chevalier, Chuck Beason and Ronnie Crawford; Falcon Club of America
- Bob Mannel; Fairlane Club of America—1962–65
- Jonathan Huntley; Fairlane Club of America—1966–69
- Howard Pardee; SAAC—Shelby Mustang
- Ned Scudder; SAAC—Shelby Cobra
- Al Aiello; insight on Falcons at Monte Carlo
- Dennis Kolodziej; complete Thunderbolt details

Acknowledgments

Writing *Fords of the Sixties* was an educational experience for me. It allowed me to learn more about a company I had spent 16 years working for and to gain inside knowledge of the leaders that made the company great. I owe many thanks to Ford Motor Company Archives, where Bonnie Walworth and Greta Krapac supported my research efforts. Detroit Library National Automotive Collection curator Mark Patrick provided access to tons of Ford advertising literature, press releases and one-of-a-kind documents to support the unique stories and information.

Joe Oros, father of the Mustang design, was a perfect gentleman and a perfect interviewee. Thanks, Joe, for your wonderful background stories about one of the world's all-time great car designs. Also, Jack Telnack, former Ford design vice president, and his teammate, Bill Shannon, provided many stories on the inner workings of Ford design during the sixties.

Auto-racing greats Dan Gurney, A. J. Foyt, Fred Lorenzen, Bob Bondurant and Carroll Shelby all spent time delivering wonderful anecdotal stories—many never in print before. I owe them each gratitude for the generosity of their time.

And I certainly owe my good friends, publishers/editors Howard and Helen Fisher and layout wizard Gary Smith, for turning the words and photos into far more than the sum of the parts. They have been wonderful to work with and deserve credit for the end result.

Having been through this exercise before when I wrote *Fords of the Fifties*, my family knew I would be spending much time away on weekends, photographing classic Fords or on the phone interviewing another legend. There were also long hours spent on the computer when I should have been watching a movie with my daughters, Erin and Allison, or taking my wife, Heidi, to dinner. They were always super-supportive, as was our fluffy watchdog, Abby, sleeping at my feet. The family is the true home support team and mine is the best.

And most important of all, I would like to dedicate this book to my father, Bill Parris, for instilling a love of fast cars in me from the start. My dad knows how to haul a '32 Ford over a gravel road at speed better than anyone I know. We bonded early on watching hot rods circle the clay at Flying Saucer Speedway and making our first trek to Daytona in 1964. Thanks, Dad. You're the greatest.

Introduction

The 1960s brought America a second decade of postwar prosperity. There was plenty to spend money on, including new cars with more advanced technologies, psychedelic clothing, color televisions and The Beatles' albums. NASCAR introduced high-banked super speedways, Indianapolis ushered in the age of rear-engined race cars and watching the Kennedys became a social pastime. The Ford family made the pages of *Life*, *Look* and *Time* on a regular basis, while the company produced some of the most notable vehicles of the century. The sixties was a period of prosperity and optimism that brought style and performance to the fore.

By the late fifties Ford Motor Company had begun planning new models for the coming decade. Exotic new body designs would be introduced each year, and horsepower would be on the rise. The early sixties brought the totally new 1960 Galaxie and the new Falcon compact. Falcon quickly became the number-one-selling compact in the United States, and the Thunderbird for 1961 set another precedent for forward styling, featuring afterburner taillights and a rocket-like front end.

By 1965, Ford's Mustang had taken the youth of the world by storm, defining a new pony car segment, later followed by GM's Camaro and Firebird and Dodge's Challenger. But Ford Motor Company, still led by Henry Ford II, was also planning a major return to motorsports, setting its sights on total victory in every major event from Daytona to Le Mans. The goal was to highlight the Total Performance sales theme. After Ford tried unsuccessfully to purchase Ferrari, he chose to make his mark with Shelby Cobras and GT40s, and would accept nothing less than complete success. At Le Mans, Daytona, Indianapolis and Baja, Ford dominated the events and welcomed all challengers.

During the sixties Ford Motor Company went head-to-head with GM and Chrysler in everything from performance to styling. Ford was building Thunderbirds that looked like jet aircraft, Mustangs that would redefine sportiness and race cars that would rattle the doors of Europe's best. Fords of the sixties would mark their place in automotive history for decades to come, and Ford Motor Company was in its glory.

▶

The 1960 Thunderbirds offered a sliding sunroof and an optional 430 cubic inch, 350 horsepower V-8. This would be the last in a series of three known as the "square birds." (Photo: Ford Motor Company)

FORD

The Year 1960

Ford designed the 1960 model in response to Chevrolet's radical 1959 styling, hoping also to sell a design that was more forward thinking. Henry Ford II wanted the new Galaxie, based on Ford's Quicksilver concept vehicle, brought to market quickly.

The 1960s saw baby boomers moving into their teenage years and starting to drive. A driver's license meant freedom, and a car was often a statement about who you were. The boomers were kicking up AM radios with the Dave Clark Five, the Grateful Dead and The Beatles. Cokes were still a nickel, gasoline was 29 cents and in-car record players were available to play 45-rpm discs—for those who could afford them. Ford was introducing a totally new Galaxie each year. The hot selling Falcon compact was killing the competition, and Mustang was the envy of the competition.

The auto industry as a whole showed a slight improvement in sales for 1960, but Ford Motor Company took a downturn, primarily in its full-size car sales. Worldwide Ford produced 2,224,859 cars and trucks in 1960, with the full-size Ford and the Thunderbird seeing substantial drops in sales, moving Ford back into second place behind Chevrolet. Falcon sales, combined with those for the Mercury Comet, pushed Ford into total compact leadership with sales of 702,117 units. The top-selling brands, Chevy and Ford, were followed on the sales charts by Plymouth, Rambler, Pontiac, Dodge and Oldsmobile.

A milestone in Ford management came in 1960 when chairman Ernie Breech retired from Ford at the July 13 meeting of the board of directors after 14 years. Breech had been hired away from GM's Bendix Division in late 1946 to mentor Henry Ford II. He also helped to guide the company out of near disaster and backed development of the 1949 sedans that saved the company. With Breech's retirement, Henry Ford II took the reins as both president and chairman. He was a man who loved his cars and his grandfather's company.

Design

Most vehicles were conceived about three years before they were actually seen by the public at a dealership. The new Falcon and Fairlane/Galaxie models were under development from 1957 to 1959 in various stages of engineering and design.

When the young designer Jack Telnack joined Ford in 1958, he started working on front grilles for the 1961 Fords. He also saw a good deal of what was happening with the '60 Ford, which was well under way by then.

Telnack says that during the 1950s and '60s it was easier to push a design through the development and approval stages more quickly than it would be in later decades. "There were a couple of reasons for that," said Telnack. "We had no government requirements, no bumper requirements, no emissions requirements. And we had far fewer models than we have today." Ford sold only three models: Falcon, Fairlane/Galaxie and Thunderbird. "It was amazing. We knew no boundaries back in those days. We didn't have the quality we have today, but it didn't matter." Style was king, and Toyota and Datsun were just beginning to bring in noticeable numbers of their new small cars. "With only three Ford models to worry about, the designers could change shapes quickly to meet market demand."

Telnack, who many years later became Ford's vice president of design, said the '60 Fairlane/Galaxie was a good example of bringing a car to market quickly. "It was the widest Ford ever built. The car was so wide that in Tennessee they actually required it to have side running lights." Telnack loved the '60 design—one of his all-time favorites. "It was based on a show car, the Quicksilver." According to Telnack, fellow designer Bill Shannon always felt the wheelbase was too long. The length apparently bothered Shannon so much that he bought a 1960 Ford, cut about a foot out of the wheelbase and drove it for several years.

Quicksilver was originally scheduled to be a 1961 show car but was brought into service much earlier than expected. Shannon shared an interesting story about how it became the 1960 Ford. He said that Fridays were "show-and-tell" days for Henry Ford II and his key executives. "Today, they talk about how it sometimes takes five years to build a car from scratch. The 1960 Ford program was done in 18 months," said Shannon. "It started Friday, March 15, 1958. There was a big [Ford design] show and everyone was in a panic." Chevrolet was bringing out a totally new design for their 1959 model, and apparently Ford had obtained a copy of the blueprints. According to Shannon, Ford built a full-scale exterior of the Chevy in the Ford design studios.

"The car was in the studio on that particular Friday along with some Ford concepts," said Shannon. "The show was upstairs in the Ford production studio. There was the mock-up of the 1959 Chevrolet and several Ford concepts, including the Quicksilver. The Quicksilver was a two-door on one side and a four-

1960 Timeline

- Introduced—The first oral contraceptive is sold at about 55 cents a pill; acetaminophen now an alternative to aspirin
- Barbra Streisand wins first talent contest in small coffee house
- Berry Gordy borrows $800 and starts Motown Records
- Alfred Hitchcock's *Psycho* a box office hit
- Lucille Ball and Desi Arnaz file for divorce
- Ernest Evans becomes "Chubby Checker"
- July 13—Ernie Breech retires as Ford board chairman
- The First Kennedy-Nixon debate draws record crowd of 75 million viewers
- Best Picture Oscar: *The Apartment* starring Jack Lemmon and Shirley MacLaine

The aerodynamic new full-size models ranged from the bottom-line Custom 300 to the Fairlane models and the top-of-the-line Galaxies. The 1960 model grew in every dimension, becoming one of the widest Ford sedans ever built.

The Starliner, one of the Galaxie family, sported a near-fastback that made it ideal for the flurry of NASCAR super speedways just opening. This gave it a major advantage over the boxy square back of the previous year. (Photos this page: Ford Motor Company)

door on the other and had a full backlight [rear glass]," he noted. "And that Friday Henry Ford II said, referring to the Quicksilver, 'Can you do this one? Can we have it?' The engineers and planning staff said, 'Yes, sir, Mr. Ford.' So that was when the whole program got under way," Shannon recalled. There was no carryover other than the underpinnings, and it was brought to market in 18 months with a two-door, four-door, wagons and Skyliner convertible.

Fairlane/Galaxie

The 1960 models were available in dealer showrooms October 8, 1959. Ford Division General Manager J. O. Wright said the new Galaxie design was originally slated for a later introduction date. "When engineers pointed out that a completely new car also would enable them to design additional quality features into the vehicle, management gave the go-ahead," said Wright.

Ford described the new design as "comfort engineering"

resulting in more hip-, shoulder-, head- and legroom. According to Wright, the new body design, new frame, redesigned suspension and improved power train gave the Ford better ride, handling and performance characteristics.

As for the Fairlane, the economy model full-size Ford for 1960, Ford advertised it as the "value leader of all big cars." You could enjoy Thunderbird styling and a choice of three Thunderbird V-8s or the Mileage Maker Six. When describing Galaxie or Fairlane features, Ford referred to Thunderbird as often as possible, hoping for a rub-off effect from their stylish flagship model.

Fairlane came with standard amenities such as rear-seat armrests, two sun visors, an extra ashtray, cigarette lighter and color-keyed steering wheel—all at no extra cost. Ford promoted the Diamond Lustre finish for no more waxing and 4,000-mile oil changes on all their 1960 car models.

The Wide-Tread design, soon to be picked up by Pontiac as

Wide-Track, provided a five-foot track, the same as Thunderbird. The rear leaf springs were a full five feet long and had anti-dive and anti-squat built into the chassis design, though Ford's claim of "sports car–like handling" was doubtful.

Motor Trend tested a 300-horsepower Starliner model, the two-door Fastback, with Cruise-O-Matic and the economy 2.91:1 rear axle in their February 1960 edition. Technical editor Chuck Nerpel recorded zero-to-60 mph at 11.7 seconds, nothing to write home about. Its top speed was 115 mph, and mileage figures ranged from 13.8 mpg in the city to 18.2 mpg on the open road.

Ford offered 13 body colors for 1960 in its Diamond Lustre finish. (Note that throughout the sixties Ford preferred using the European spelling of "litre" and "lustre," hoping to bring a touch of class to its products.)

The standard engine was a 145 horsepower Mileage Maker Six, a 223 cubic inch I-6 using a single-barrel carburetor and regular fuel.

The Starliner's rounded front and sloping roofline helped it to cut through the air at tracks like Daytona and Charlotte in NASCAR stock car racing.

The open-air Sunliner was a sensation among U.S. convertibles, with its exceptional style and power. For customers wanting to burn a little rubber with the roof down, a 300 horsepower 352 cubic inch Thunderbird Special V-8 was available.

Sunliner convertible prices started at $2,973.

Sunliner was one of the all-time best designs according to retired Ford Design Vice President Jack Telnack.

1960 Galaxie Sunliner

Optional engines for the full-size models were the 185 horsepower Thunderbird 292 V-8, a 235 horsepower Thunderbird 352 V-8, the 300 horsepower Thunderbird 352 V-8 and the limited production 360 horsepower 352 Super V-8. The 360 horse version came with a 9.6:1 compression ratio, a special four-barrel carburetor, solid lifters and low-restriction dual exhausts.

Transmissions were the standard three-speed column-mounted manual shift; the two-speed Fordomatic, available with all engines but the Super V-8; and the Cruise-O-Matic, available on all but the Mileage Maker Six.

1960 Ford Options

300 hp 352 V-8	177.40
Cruise-O-Matic	211.10
Fordomatic	179.80
Overdrive	108.40
Equa-Lock differential	38.60
Master-Guide power steering	76.50
Power brakes	43.20
4-way power seat	63.80
Power lift windows	102.10
SelectAire conditioner	403.80
Console Range radio	58.50

Falcon

Falcon was an important entry into the Ford lineup, becoming the third best-selling car in the industry and best in its class in its first year. It sold more than the Chevy Corvair and Plymouth Valiant combined.

All the major manufacturers were introducing compact models, and Ford wanted to be the major player. The company had considered a small car since the early 1950s but felt the time just wasn't right for a successful launch. In 1954 Ford had market research done that indicated that only 5 percent of the American public was interested in small cars. This still wasn't enough for them to build one, but it did encourage them to put a team of young market researchers in place to find out customer preferences if Ford were to build a small car.

Ford's marketing research manager, Dr. George Brown, directed the 1954 market research involving 2,000 interviews. He then organized them by coding the replies and putting them on punch cards for one of the earliest computerized analyses of this type. Ford found that the most important features a potential small-car owner wanted was gasoline economy, economical maintenance and operation, and low purchase price.

Ford Division's product planning manager Will Scott said, "The basic problem with designing an economy car was to get three-quarters of a ton of weight out of it. You have to get rid of weight to get gas economy, and you have to get rid of weight to cut cost." He said one way to cut weight was to cut the number of cylinders in the engine. They decided on using a six-cylinder to keep the short-stroke smoothness that they felt a four-cylinder would not provide. The goal was to provide a compact car that delivered to the customer at 2,350 pounds.

By 1957 Ford development was well under way for an October 1959 launch of the new compact. Henry Ford II revealed the car to the press on September 2, 1959, via a closed-circuit television conference from Dearborn to 21 cities around the country. He and company chairman Ernie Breech said the new Falcon would be a six-passenger, six-cylinder, 90 horsepower vehicle capable of attaining 30 miles per gallon. Henry Ford II also said he thought an affordable compact would help to accelerate the increase in multiple-car families.

On September 10, eight days later, 16 Falcons left Dearborn on the first lap of a "quarter-million mile experience run," according to the *Rouge News,* Ford's employee newspaper. Two of the Falcons were to make daily runs on the turnpikes between Chicago and New York, and the remaining 14 vehicles were to cover every mile of federally numbered highways in the continental United States. "This would make Falcon the most tested automobile to reach the American market," it noted.

At introduction, Falcon was 40 percent lighter than the full-size Ford, weighing in at 2,366 pounds and more than two feet shorter. Yet the front legroom was only one-tenth of an inch shorter and headroom actually increased.

The Falcon was built on a 109-inch wheelbase and came only with a 144 cubic-inch I-6 engine, producing 90 horsepower.

Ford advertising promoted Falcon as America's lowest priced six-passenger car: "To be exact, the Falcon is priced up to $124 less than other six-passenger cars in the compact car field. And this is just the start of your savings. The Falcon gets up to 30 miles per gallon on regular gas and 4,000 miles between oil changes." Falcon also came standard with a "double-life" aluminized muffler, a Diamond Lustre finish that never needed waxing and, according to Ford, "power brakes and steering were totally unnecessary" so Falcon was again saving buyers money. Ford claimed in their ads that a buyer could save up to 15 percent on insurance, and service was simple and inexpensive, making it "the easiest car in the world to own."

Another interesting Falcon advertising tactic to counter the crosstown rival, Corvair, was placing hard-hitting magazine and newspaper ads. "The engine is up front to reduce chances of oversteering [characteristic of many rear-engine cars], or skidding out of control in emergency stops." Ads also noted that "the gas tank is safely in the rear, instead of up front 'in the laps' of driver and front-seat passengers."

The rounded front features of the 1960 Galaxie helped to give it a soft, aerodynamic look.

The trunk space was mammoth, although somewhat shallow.

With one of Ford's widest ever bodies, the Sunliner's bench seat could accommodate three across with room to spare.

More than 44,000 Sunliners were sold during the model year.

The flat fins across the rear deck accentuated the Galaxie's width.

1960 Galaxie Sunliner

1960 Ford Country Squire Wagon

Quad headlamps would still be in fashion for some time to come.

Ford safety features for 1960 included a collapsible steering wheel, stronger safety locks and a padded instrument panel.

The wagons used the same 120 mph speedometers as the high-performance models.

Power brakes were a $43 option and power steering was an additional $77.

With all rear seats folded down the wagons provided a huge cargo area.

Small chrome ornamentation graced all full-size Ford fenders.

The six-passenger, six-cylinder Ranch Wagon started at $2,656.

The two vehicles were so different that the customer interested in the Falcon probably would not have been interested in the Corvair anyway.

Falcon owners loved the car's economy, looks, riding comfort and handling ease. But they almost always mentioned the lack of power in the 144 cubic inch I-6 engine.

Motor Trend scored it against its primary competitors, Valiant and Corvair, and found the Falcon to have the best quality, gas mileage and trunk space of the three. But it fell short against the others in power, ease of city driving and smoothness of ride on poor roads.

Although advertised as getting as much as 30 miles per gallon, Falcon road tests regularly showed the average to be closer to 20 mpg. Offered in a two-door and four-door sedan, wagon and Ranchero pickup, Falcon was a huge sales success, selling almost 460,000 units during its first year on the market.

The Falcon chassis also lived on to become the basis of the Mustang four years later.

Ford added the Falcon Ranchero to the lineup later in the year, bringing back the car/pickup format of the 1957–59 Galaxie-bodied Rancheros.

At a base price of $1,862, the Falcon Ranchero was the first compact truck to be marketed by a major U.S. manufacturer. The payload capacity was 800 pounds and it would seat three across with the bench seat configuration. Ford used a zinc coating on many of the underbody parts to resist corrosion, and bolt-on fenders were a part of the ease-of-repair design. Ranchero's six-foot bed was only 21.6 inches from the ground, making it easy to load cargo. Almost everything was optional, such as a radio, safety belts, windshield washer, and heater. A 90 horsepower I-6 was standard power.

1960 Falcon Options

Fordomatic	159.40
Fresh air heater	67.80
Deluxe trim	65.80
Push-button radio	54.05
Aquamatic windshield washer	13.70
Whitewall tires	28.70
Padded sun visors	19.20

Thunderbird

The 1960 Thunderbird was the last of a three-year run for the four-seat model. Although the body was basically the same, the body side moldings and grille work were changed. Thunderbird also offered a completely automatic soft top for the convertible and an all-new sunroof. The latter was offered for buyers who "prefer hardtop styling, but enjoy the open air benefits of a convertible." The all-steel sliding roof panel was a $212 option for the '60 model, riding on aluminum glides and opened by a hand-operated crank.

The convertible soft top was improved for 1960, with a completely automatic top that would fold beneath the deck lid without infringing on rear passengers' seating space. Without a snap-on boot, the Thunderbird convertible had a clean, smooth appearance.

The new front-end treatment featured an aluminum mesh grille and a larger one-piece bumper. The rear of the Thunderbird had a freshened arrangement for the taillights, with three per side and the addition of chrome vertical hash bars on each rear quarter panel.

Horsepower was another boost in Thunderbird's quest for performance, with the addition of a 430 cubic inch, 350 horsepower V-8. With 490 ft.-lbs. of torque, it would launch even this 4,410-pound sports luxury model at a snappy rate of acceleration. Zero-to-60 mph was recorded at 8.9 seconds by *Motor Trend* magazine. According to the *Motor Trend* staff writers, this just barely classified

the car as being in the "hot class." They suggested acceleration could have been substantially improved by changing to a performance axle from the standard 3.10:1. Gas mileage averaged around 12 mpg with the big-block option. *Motor Trend* writers also suggested that the T-Bird "has never been the good handling car that drivers expect from a vehicle of such sporty appearance." But, with a plush ride and a weight of well more than two tons, its lack of good handling characteristics was really no surprise.

1960 Thunderbird Options

430 Special V-8	177.00
Cruise-O-Matic	242.00
Master-Guide power steering	75.30
Swift Sure power brakes	43.20
Power driver's seat	92.10
Central console radio	112.80
SelectAire conditioner	465.80
Sliding sunroof	212.40
Leather upholstery	106.20

Looking Forward

By the end of the model year, Ford was rushing a new 1961 model Galaxie design to market, along with an all-new Thunderbird and a carryover Falcon. Ford wanted to play it a bit safer, the formula that had made Falcon a success, by making Galaxie more conservative, a design that more middle-class Americans could relate to. While 1960 wasn't as profitable as 1959, it was still respectable, and Henry just wanted to make certain that each Ford model could compete with the best in each segment.

Ford Engines for 1960

CID	Carb.	Comp.	HP
144 I-6	1 bbl	8.7	90 @ 4200
223 I-6	1 bbl	8.4	145 @ 4000
292 V-8	2 bbl	8.8	185 @ 4200
352 V-8	2 bbl	8.9	220 @ 4300
352 V-8	4 bbl	9.6	300 @ 4600
352 V-8	4 bbl	9.6	360 @ 4800
430 V-8	4 bbl	10.1	350 @ 4800

Falcon styling was far more conservative than the Chevrolet Corvair, but apparently the public liked it. Falcon outsold the Corvair and the Plymouth Valiant combined.

Falcon Ranchero was sold as a truck but was purchased mostly by car owners as a weekend cargo hauler.

The Falcon Tudor wagon wasn't nearly as popular as the four-door, with only 27,552 being produced. (Photos this page: Ford Motor Company)

The last year for the square T-Bird body style saw few changes, although it offered the first Ford sunroof option.

1960 Car Production

Falcon

Fordor Sedan	167,896
Tudor Sedan	193,470
Fordor Wagon	46,758
Tudor Wagon	27,552
Sedan Delivery	2,374
Ranchero	21,027

Ford Fairlane

4-door Sedan	109,801
2-door Sedan	93,259
2-door Business Sedan	1,733

Ford Fairlane 500

4-door Sedan	153,234
2-door Sedan	91,041

Ford Deluxe

Custom 300 2-door Sedan	572
Custom 300 4-door Sedan	302

Ford Galaxie

4-door Sedan	104,784
2-door Sedan	31,866
4-door Victoria	39,215
2-door Victoria Starliner	68,641
Sunliner Convertible	44,762

Ford Station Wagons

4-door Ranch Wagon	43,872
2-door Ranch Wagon	27,136
Country Sedan 6-passenger	59,302
Country Sedan 9-passenger	19,277
Country Squire	22,237

Thunderbird

2-door Hardtop	78,447
Convertible	11,860
2-door Gold Top	2,536
Total	**1,462,954**

Thunderbird stylists planted triple taillights at the rear, an aluminum mesh grille up front and vertical hash bars on the rear quarter panels. The rest of the car stayed basically the same. (Photos this page: Ford Motor Company)

This would add up to profits, and he was keenly aware of his stockholders' need for a return on their investment in Ford.

Ford and all other major manufacturers would be pushing ahead with development of their compact car lines. In 1960, U.S.-produced com-pacts accounted for 25 percent of the market, more than 2½ times the 1959 rate for compact sales. Ford Motor Company had also invested more than $128 million in its manufacturing facilities in 1960, assuring that by March 1961 most of its plants would be able to produce more than one line of vehicles.

The Levacar concept was designed to "ride on air," according to Ford Design Vice President George Walker. This was an auto-show-only display vehicle. Ford said that Levacar was supposed to attain speeds of up to 200 mph on a thin bed of air. (Photo: Ford Motor Company)

Robert McNamara was elected president of Ford in November 1960 but lasted only three months in the position before President Kennedy tapped him for Secretary of Defense, leaving Henry once again as president and CEO. Although it was an honor to have one of Ford's Whiz Kids picked for this position, Ford was still in need of a talented president, and Henry didn't want the job.

The company appeared to be on the right track to regain any losses from slow 1960 Galaxie sales, continue growing the healthy compact models and deliver an all new Thunderbird for 1961. Henry pointed out in his closing statement to stockholders that "American freedom and American opportunity are the silent partners of every business in the land, and your company can look to the future with full expectation of continued success."

Concept Cars

Concepts were popular in the 1950s, and in 1960 Ford took its Levacar floating vehicle to the Design for Suburban Living show at Redondo Beach, California. The vehicle was designed to float on a thin layer of air while being driven forward by a small gasoline engine powering a fan. The vehicle had first been introduced in 1958 at Ford's Rotunda and seemed to gain popularity because of the idea that it could make the wheel obsolete.

At the California display, the 650-pound Levacar floated using an outside air source for levitation. You might say the idea never really got off the ground, but it managed to get plenty of hype from the Ford public relations department and the national press.

1960 Model Car Pricing

Falcon

Tudor Sedan I-6	$1,912
Fordor Sedan I-6	$1,974

Fairlane

2-door Business Sedan I-6	$2,170
4-door Town Sedan I-6	$2,311

Fairlane 500

2-door Club Sedan I-6	$2,334
4-door Town Sedan I-6	$2,388

Galaxie

2-door Club Sedan I-6	$2,549
4-door Town Sedan I-6	$2,603
4-door Town Victoria I-6	$2,675
2-door Starliner I-6	$2,610
Sunliner Convertible I-6	$2,860

Station Wagons

Ranch Wagon 6-passenger I-6	$2,586
Country Squire 9-passenger V-8	$2,967

Thunderbird

Hardtop	$3,755
Convertible	$4,222

▶

With slower sales from the 1960 models, Ford decided to try a more conservative approach to styling for the 1961 Galaxie. They went back to the traditional round taillights and added more traditional rear fins. (Photo: Ford Motor Company)

FORD

The Year 1961

With sales of the 1960 models down, more conservative styling was introduced for 1961. The 1961 Sunliner convertible with a V-8 started at $2,963 and was considerably more maneuverable, with a smaller exterior package.

New Ford products for 1961 included Thunderbird and another all new body design for the full-size Ford. The Falcon was still climbing in sales with fresh versions including the sporty Futura model. Ford also made safety belt attachments standard in all its cars, allowing seat belts to be installed safely by a dealer or car owner after production.

Business at Ford was good in what was a slow year for most manufacturers. With total industry sales declining 15.2 percent below the previous year, Ford actually gained market share, moving from 26.3 percent to 28.7 percent of total industry sales.

Ford's Falcon, Thunderbird and Mercury Comet all established retail sales records, and Ford Motor Company would have moved even more cars had it not been for a labor strike during the new model introduction. Henry Ford II told stockholders, "Dealers were left with an insufficient inventory of new models at a time of strong customer demand." Even with substantial overtime in production, Ford could not catch up with dealer orders for the new vehicles. Ford still managed to sell more than two million cars and trucks, down more than 8 percent from 1960, and the new three-year union contract provided some assurance of uninterrupted production for the near future.

In 1961 Henry II was still running the company and Lee Iacocca was appointed General Manager of Ford Division, continuing his rise to power. Iacocca would be laying the groundwork for the future performance and sports model vehicles including Mustang. He came into this position after the success of the Falcon and was setting his sights on the Mustang pony car that would come just three years later. His tenure as head of the division was one of the high points in his career, as he made it to the corporate vice president level before turning 40. The young executive would make his mark early on, providing healthy profits for the company during the rest of the decade.

Putting pressure on the competition, Ford Motor Company decided to offer an industry standard beating warranty of 12,000 miles or 12 months—whichever came first. "No other American automobile carries a warranty like this," said Henry Ford II. The previous Ford warranty was only 4,000 miles or three months. Ford said every 1961 model in its lineup was styled, designed, engineered and manufactured with three primary goals in mind: finest quality, greatest durability and most reliable operation. A warranty this long would provide customers with the confidence to buy a new Ford without worry. The rest of the industry soon followed suit.

Trying to expand and diversify their business, in 1961 Ford acquired partial assets of the Electric Autolite Company and all of Philco to expand their participation in the replacement parts market and the electronics and space fields. The government stepped in and sued Ford for antitrust violations even though GM had its own in-house Delco sparkplug industry. Nevertheless, Ford moved ahead and owned Autolite for several years before the suit went to trial. They finally ended up turning the business into the current-day Motorcraft brand.

Engines

The star of the Ford engine family for 1961 was the 390 V-8, derived from the 352 V-8. It produced 300 hp at 4,600 rpm, matching power in the high-performance 352 from 1960. The 390 had more torque than the 300 hp 352 and, according to *Motor Trend* writer John Lawlor, the new engine was stronger.

In a December 1960 article Lawlor said, "The greater displacement and higher torque of the new 390 suggest that it's a significantly more powerful unit. My own suspicion is the 352 was rated optimistically while the 390 produces closer to an honest 300 horsepower."

Later in the year Ford offered the 390 with higher compression and three two-barrel carburetors producing 401 horsepower, the most potent V-8 ever offered in a high-volume production Ford.

The Ford engine lineup included the 144 and 170 I-6 for Falcon, and the 223 I-6, 292 V-8, 352 V-8 and the new 390 V-8 available in all full-size Fords. Thunderbird came standard with the 300 horsepower 390 V-8 only.

Custom 300/Fairlane/Galaxie

The full-size Fords for 1961 still included the Galaxie, Fairlane, Fairlane 500 and the base Custom 300 models. The Starliner and Sunliner series were now a part of the Galaxie family, and all models enjoyed longer intervals between service appointments. Ford recommended 20,000 to 30,000 miles between lubrications and 4,000 miles between oil changes. Ford also made self-adjusting brakes standard on the big models, keeping owners from having to visit the dealer too often.

The Starliner model sold only 29,669 units in 1961, with most two-door buyers choosing the square B-pillar look of the Galaxie

Club Victoria, which sold 75,437 units. The moneymaker of the big Fords was still the Galaxie four-door sedan, finding 141,823 buyers. Priced from $2,590 for the six-cylinder to $2,706 for the V-8, it had good looks, value and utility for the buyers Ford was after.

1961 Timeline

- Henry Ford II resumes duties as president of Ford
- Russians send first man into space
- Bay of Pigs invasion of Cuba fails
- Berlin Wall goes up
- The twist craze begins
- Minimum wage becomes $1.15 per hour
- Robert Zimmerman sings in Greenwich Village nightclub as "Bob Dylan"
- Best Picture Oscar: *West Side Story* starring Natalie Wood

The Galaxie Club Victoria (top) and the Galaxie Starliner were trimmed down 3.7 inches shorter and 1.6 inches narrower than the 1960 models they replaced. Both were available with a new 390 cubic inch V-8 producing 300 horsepower. (Photos this page: Ford Motor Company)

1961 Ford Galaxie

Angled fins were back in for 1961, with more traditional styling overall.

The 1961 front end design was simpler and more conservative than in the previous model.

Galaxie's trunk remained spacious, but most luggage had to be laid on its side due to a lack of depth.

The midyear introduction of a triple two-barrel 390 V-8 with 401 horsepower was a rare option, with only a handful actually seeing

The 1961 Galaxie models featured self-adjusting brakes and intervals of

1961 Ford Galaxie Starliner

Ford shrank the Galaxie body dimensions in both width and length in 1961, thinking they had gone too far with the size of the 1960 models.

The new Galaxie Starliner started at $2,713 with a V-8 engine.

The Starliner roofline helped Ford stay competitive in NASCAR during the 1961 season.

The 1961 models were quieter, as Ford started using butyl rubber for body mounts. To keep the ride smooth, semi-elliptical rear springs with thinner main leaves were used on all body types except for the two-door and hardtop models. Ford also studied the weak points of the 1960 chassis and made changes including a lighter frame and more rigid body panels to cut down on resonance and vibration.

Compared to the 1960 models, exterior body dimensions were downsized. The 1961 Galaxies were 3.7 inches shorter and 1.6 inches narrower than the 1960 full-size models. The wheelbase stayed at 119 inches and the height remained at 55 inches. The new Ford had a higher hood line, a full-width grille and more defined side panels. The hood opening was 11 inches narrower, helping to form a more rigid assembly but also making

The 1961 model Fords used simulated grille work between the large, round taillights. Small, angular fins were also back after a one-year absence.

The big news for 1961 was the Thunderbird. The all-new rocket styling featured afterburner taillights and a standard 390 cubic inch V-8. The roof still folded seamlessly into the trunk on convertible models, leaving little luggage space.

The Thunderbird came standard with bucket seats, a hot V-8, and a Diamond Lustre paint finish that, according to Ford, "never needs waxing." (Photos this page: Ford Motor Company)

for tighter access to the engine for repairs. Ford reduced the overhang at the rear and made the trunk opening larger. The spare tire was moved toward the backseat, making it easier to load luggage or cargo.

Wagons now had a more squared-off rear end, and the lift gate was replaced with a roll-down window. A manual crank operated the window on the less-expensive models, but the Country Squire came standard with an electric switch for its gate window.

1961 Ford Options

300 hp 390 V-8	196.70
Fordomatic transmission	179.80
Cruise-O-Matic	212.30
Equa-Lock differential	38.60
Power steering	81.70
Power brakes	43.20
SelectAire conditioner	436.00
Power windows	102.10
4-way power front seat	63.80

Thunderbird

Thunderbird was new inside and out for 1961. The high-end Ford model never carried the Ford name or badge but was often a harbinger of things to come on other models. It followed the traditional three-year styling run with the two-seater first, then the square-bird look and now the rocket-bird.

Ford Engines for 1961			
CID	Carb.	Comp.	HP
144 I-6	1 bbl	8.7	85 @ 4200
170 I-6	1 bbl	8.7	101 @ 4400
223 I-6	1 bbl	8.4	135 @ 4000
292 V-8	2 bbl	8.8	175 @ 4200
352 V-8	2 bbl	8.9	220 @ 4400
390 V-8	4 bbl	9.6	300 @ 4600
390 V-8	4 bbl	9.6	330 @ 5000
390 V-8	4 bbl	11.1	375 @ 6000
390 V-8	3x2 bbl	11.1	401 @ 6000

Ford hoped to garner a touch of Italian flair with their 1961 styling by photographing their new Galaxie in Rome.

The overall Thunderbird concept was still focused on personal luxury with strong performance and seating for four. The controversial styling was evidently a love-it or hate-it affair with potential buyers, and sales actually dropped from more than 92,000 in 1960 to around 73,000 for the new model. The new body, described by Thunderbird designer Bill Boyer as having "projectile styling," had features that seemed to spring from jet aircraft. It had afterburner taillights, delicate fins and an aggressive wedge front end. Thunderbird had become the company's flagship, influencing other Ford models a year or two later. The bucket seats and console found in the 1958–60 models were now showing up in the Falcon Futura and Galaxie models, and almost every V-8 in the Ford lineup was tagged with the Thunderbird name, even though only one of them was actually offered in the 'Bird.

When asked to come up with a new T-Bird series, designers presented two early proposals to management for approval. Elwood Engle from the Advanced Design Studio and Bill Boyer from the Ford Studio competed with their design teams. Engle's version, a long, sleek model with rounded corners, was tapped by Ford executive Robert McNamara as the next Lincoln Continental. It would be transformed from a two-door into a four-door luxury sedan and convertible. Boyer's version was chosen as the basis for

the new Thunderbird because it was considered more youthful and forward looking. As it turned out, both models were eventually built on the same line at the Wixom Assembly Plant in Michigan.

The interior design team was led by Art Querfeld. The new interior had a full wraparound console that flowed from the dash to the rear seats. There were plenty of smooth lines, brushed aluminum and an array of gauges for the driver. The vinyl-covered front seats provided plenty of legroom, and the individual backseats were roomy enough to carry adults on short trips. The new swing-away steering wheel provided easy entry and exit and, once in place, it would also telescope to fit the driver.

Ford had considered a front-wheel-drive format for the new Thunderbird early on, but decided that it would cause undue wear on the brakes, tires and U-joints, leading to increased warranty costs. Front-wheel-drive would also have allowed for a flat front floorboard, but much of the attractiveness of the 'Bird came from the console and wraparound feel of the cockpit. So the project was dropped as it appeared not to add value for the buyer.

1961 Thunderbird Options

Equa-Lock differential	38.60
Whitewall rayon tires	42.10
Power lift windows	102.10
Power driver's seat	92.10
SelectAire conditioner	498.00
Push-button radio	112.80
Tinted glass	43.00
Outside mirror	5.10

Falcon

In 1961 Falcons had a new convex aluminum grille and an optional 101 hp 170 cubic inch I-6 engine. The standard I-6 dropped from 90 to 85 horsepower, delivering up to 30 mpg according to Ford. Two- and four-door models were available on both sedans and wagons, and an all-new Sedan Delivery model was added to the lineup, replacing the bigger Courier model. The Falcon Ranchero was still basically unchanged, selling 20,937 units. Ranchero was counted as a truck and therefore not included in overall Falcon production numbers.

With Falcon prices ranging from $1,912 to $2,268, Ford's compact competitors from Japan were lower priced but still perceived as offering less value. The Datsun Bluebird sedan

1961 Ford Falcon

Still holding the line with a base price of $1,912, Falcon was viewed by the public as an affordable compact with clean styling. It totaled an attractive value for Middle America. With a new convex grille and optional 101 horsepower I-6 engine, Falcon continued its staggering success, topping 1960 sales.

started at $1,616 and Toyota's Tiara started at $1,613, but neither was yet a threat to the hot-selling Ford compact.

Falcon's interior came with a spacious bench seat in most models, and the interior was designed to provide plenty of headroom in the front and rear seating positions. A three-speed column-mounted manual gearbox came standard, and a two-speed Fordomatic was available at extra cost.

Ford was selling Falcons at a high rate in 1961. By the end of February, Falcon accounted for an amazing 9.3 percent of total domestic car sales in the United States and was already 14,000 units ahead of Corvair. It would finish the year with a new record total production of 497,166 units, almost 40,000 more than its record first year.

Economy was one of Falcon's bragging points in advertising and public relations, so Ford entered the compact in events that would highlight how inexpensive it was

to own the vehicle. In March 1961, Falcons placed first and second in the Mobil Economy Run covering 2,500 miles from Los Angeles to Chicago. The winner bested 63 other entries, averaging 32.68 mpg. The second-place vehicle, also a Falcon, averaged 31.62 mpg. This supported Ford claims that with the standard 85 horsepower engine, Falcon could attain 30 mpg under normal driving conditions.

The new Falcon Futura was introduced on April 1, 1961, and started a midyear introduction trend for Ford. The company liked to describe the Futura as a personalized family car, "a compact cousin of the Thunderbird." Iacocca said the new model Falcon would be displayed for the first time at the New York Auto Show and would be in dealer showrooms by mid-April. "We are introducing the Falcon Futura for compact car buyers who want to combine luxury appearance with economical operation," said Iacocca.

1961 Model Car Pricing

Falcon

Tudor Sedan	$1,912
Futura 2-door	$2,160
Fordor Wagon	$2,268

Fairlane

Club Sedan 4-door I-6	$2,261
Town Sedan 4-door V-8	$2,431

Fairlane 500

Club Sedan 2-door I-6	$2,376
Club Sedan 4-door V-8	$2,492

Custom 300

4-door Sedan I-6	$2,284
2-door Sedan I-6	$2,230

Galaxie

Town Sedan 4-door I-6	$2,590
Starliner 2-door I-6	$2,597
Sunliner Convertible I-6	$2,847
Town Sedan 4-door V-8	$2,706
Starliner 2-door V-8	$2,713
Sunliner Convertible V-8	$2,963

Station Wagons

Ranch Wagon 6-passenger I-6	$2,656
Country Sedan 9-passenger V-8	$2,972
Country Squire 9-passenger V-8	$3,127

Thunderbird

Coupe	$4,170
Convertible	$4,637

Econoline was new for 1961, offered in panel van, passenger van and pickup versions. Ford again outsold its Chevy Corvair competitor by keeping everything simple, including a front-mounted I-6 engine with rear drive. Ford learned early on that the market for a low-priced van equated simplicity with dependability. (Photo: Ford Motor Company)

1961 Car Production

Fairlane 500
4-door Sedan	98,917
2-door Sedan	42,468

Falcon
Fordor Sedan	159,761
Tudor Sedan	149,982
2-door Futura Sedan	44,470
2-door Economy Sedan	50
Fordor Wagon	87,933
Tudor Wagon	32,045
Sedan Delivery	1,988
Ranchero	20,937

Custom 300
4-door	303
2-door	49

Fairlane
4-door	96,602
2-door	66,875

Galaxie
4-door Sedan	141,823
2-door Sedan	27,780

Galaxie Victoria
4-door Town Victoria	30,342
2-door Club Victoria	75,437
2-door Starliner	29,669
Sunliner Convertible	44,614

Station Wagons
4-door Ranch Wagon	30,292
2-door Ranch Wagon	12,042
4-door Country Sedan, 9-passenger	16,356
4-door Country Sedan, 6-passenger	46,311
Country Squire 9-passenger	14,657
Country Squire 6-passenger	16,961

Thunderbird
2-door Hardtop	62,535
2-door Convertible	10,516
Total	**1,361,715**

The Futura models had an array of standard features not found on the other models, including armrests, front and rear ashtrays, bucket seats and console, vinyl seat covers, "wall-to-wall" deep pile carpeting and unique wheel covers. The bucket seats were foam padded and individually adjustable, while the rear bench had indentations to suggest seating for two not three across.

All Futura models were built at the Lorain, San Jose, Kansas City and Atlanta assembly plants.

1961 Falcon Options

Falcon 170 Special I-6	37.40
Fordomatic	163.10
Manual radio	54.05
Deluxe trim package	78.30
PolarAire conditioner	262.00
Windshield washer	13.70
Whitewall tires	29.90
Fresh air heater/defroster	73.40
Power tailgate window (wagons)	29.75

Econoline

Ford introduced the Econoline economy truck line in mid-1961 to compete with small imported trucks. The model line included a pickup, van and eight-passenger Station Bus. All were mounted on a 90-inch wheelbase and equipped with a 144 cubic inch I-6 Falcon engine. The engine, mounted between the front seats, was insulated to separate the driver and passengers from both heat and excess engine noise. The 85 horsepower six-cylinder was designed to provide dependable, economical power.

"Econoline units carry a volume and load comparable to conventional pickup or panel trucks," said Ford Truck General Manager Wilbur Chase, "yet have far less weight, greater maneuverability and offer much better economy." Econoline was almost two feet shorter than the Falcon station wagon. Nearly everything came as an option, including a heater, radio, side door, sun visors, and outside mirrors.

The new small-truck line was successful, selling 15,082 Falcon Econoline buses and 46,053 Econoline pickups and vans.

Concept Cars

Ford introduced the Gyron concept car in 1961, although it had been in various stages of design since 1956 under designer Alex Tremulis. It evolved from a four-wheel model to a two-wheeler with a built-in gyroscope used as a stabilizer. The Gyron was finished

The Gyron concept car was a Ford study of space-age influence on the automotive industry. The non-operational concept was "an outstanding example of visioneering that is the heart of progressive automobile styling," according to Ford Design Vice President George Walker. (Photo: Ford Motor Company)

by a number of stylists from the Advanced Studio under the direction of Elwood Engle. The futuristic concept was supposed to be the answer to General Motors' Firebird III "laboratory on wheels." While somewhat ahead of his time, Tremulis believed that all cars would eventually have to be designed around an aerodynamic body style, and he hoped to incorporate the gyroscopic stabilizer in cars, trains and other vehicles. Ford Motor Company didn't see the Gyron as anything more than a show car displaying a futuristic design, and it was the last concept introduced before George Walker's retirement.

Walker believed in having his designers always dream about the future and often promoted what he felt might be in store for the automotive industry in coming decades. "We have reached the conclusion that very few ideas," said Walker, "are so fanciful as to be completely outside the realm of possibility." In a 1960 *Ford Rouge News* article he predicted future highways might take on another form or not exist at all. The car of the future might travel on land, sea and air and could be powered by gasoline or by a compact, long-life atomic capsule. While these ideas haven't made much progress since Walker's days, most manufacturers are working on hybrid electric and fuel cell systems while gasoline-powered highway vehicles still rule the market.

Looking Forward

With 1961 winding down, Ford was preparing for an onslaught of new product introductions in the fall. Dealers were still helping keep the new designs a secret by soaping the showroom windows and covering the cars until introduction day. The Ford executive chain was continuing to change along with the car designs. In Dearborn, George Walker's tenure was about to end with his retirement and a new era of design under Gene Bordinat would soon begin. Henry II was still fully in command and appeared to be bringing Lee Iacocca up the corporate ladder to the presidency. The decade would be one of Ford's most exciting, with great cars, charismatic personalities and racing champions all playing a role in the company's history.

▶

Ford considered introducing a bolt-on hardtop for the convertible, primarily to give its stock car teams something more aerodynamic to race with. NASCAR wouldn't approve it. (Photo: Ford Motor Company)

FORD

The Year 1962

By 1962 Ford was showing off in every segment sport models featuring bucket seats, high-horsepower V-8 engines and four-on-the-floor.

Worldwide sales for Ford in 1962 were healthy. The company had record sales of more than U.S. $8 billion, more than 18 percent higher than the previous record in 1957 and 21 percent higher than 1961. Factory sales of cars and trucks from the U.S. Ford plants totaled 2,303,850 units—some 277,000 units more than the previous year. The record production year was still 1955 at 2,613,195 cars and trucks; however, the net profit for 1962 was a record $481 million. The company was producing products the public wanted, and the profits were rolling in.

Ford spent $280 million to modernize its facilities across the States and planned to increase dramatically the spending beyond its borders for 1963. Ford was selling more than a million vehicles in other countries now and wanted to continue growing that business, seeing Europe and South America as serious profit centers.

Ford lost one of its landmarks, the Rotunda, on November 9, 1962, from a flash fire started while workers were waterproofing the roof. The famous Ford display, known as the Gateway to the Rouge, had been moved from Chicago to Dearborn after the 1936 World's Fair. The building was used to feature new Ford products, holiday displays, a Teflon "ice rink" and a car test track re-

creating surfaces from 17 famous roads around the world. The steel and limestone structure's dome roof caved in under the extreme heat and destroyed the building. Fortunately, no one was seriously injured in the disaster. Most of the company's extensive archives in the north wing of the building were saved, including 450,000 photographs.

Just two months prior to the fire, Ford employees were invited to the September 9–10 new car preview for the 1962 models at the Rotunda. Employees were allowed to bring their families for an advance peek at what Ford would be showing to the public. With more than 20 new 1962 models on display, the company enjoyed the chance to give its employees this preview so that they would spread the word about the coming products to their neighbors.

The big product news for 1962 was Ford's first mid-size car, the Fairlane. The successful name was passed on to give the new vehicle some instant recognition for customers. Scheduled to hit dealer showrooms on September 29 along with the Fairlane was a new

Galaxie 500 and mildly freshened Falcon. Thunderbird, while not significantly different from the previous year, now offered a Sports Roadster convertible model and a new Landau hardtop with a vinyl roof.

Engines

Ford introduced two new engines for 1962. The new 406 cubic inch V-8 was strictly for the high-performance and racing enthusiast, and the Challenger 221 and 260 V-8s were designed specifically for the new mid-size Fairlane entry.

The 406 V-8 replaced the high-performance 390 V-8 models from the year before. The 390 CIDs, with 375 and 401 horsepower, were dropped after early 1962 when the 406 V-8 was announced. The new power plant was based on the 390 V-8 block and produced 385 horsepower with a single four-barrel carburetor and 405 horsepower with a three two-barrel version. The 406 V-8 was available in all full-size models except the wagons.

The small-block 221 and 260 cubic inch V-8 engines were

1962 Timeline

- K-Mart, Diet Rite are introduced
- Ford builds thirty millionth V-8 July 2
- November 9—fire destroys the Ford Rotunda building after 18 million visitors
- John Glenn is first American to orbit the earth
- U.S.S.R. "blinks" in Cuban Missile Crisis
- Best Picture Oscar: *Lawrence of Arabia* starring Peter O'Toole

The 1962 Ford Sunliner could be ordered with a 406 V-8, 401 horsepower and a console-mounted four-speed transmission. The soft top was fully automatic.

completely new from the ground up. Both were available only with a two-barrel carburetor, producing 145 and 164 horsepower respectively. This new family of small-block V-8s was snappier and less thirsty than the older 292 V-8 used in the full-size Fords, and fit snugly into the Fairlane's engine compartment. The 221 V-8 could be bought with an automatic overdrive planetary fourth gear. This cut the rpm by 28 percent to assist in overall highway mileage. The 260 cubic inch version was introduced in the Fairlane 500 at the February Chicago Auto Show.

The standard Fairlane engine was the familiar 170 cubic inch, 101 horsepower six-cylinder. The overhead valve six used Ford's short-stroke design, providing excellent horsepower at higher rpm but with less low-end torque. This engine was the optional Falcon power plant.

All engines from the Mileage Maker Six to the 352 V-8 were available with Fordomatic, the popular two-speed automatic. Ford's heavy-duty Cruise-O-Matic, the three-speed automatic, was available on any of the V-8 engines except the new 406 V-8.

Manual shifts were available on any engine, and a floor-mounted four-speed was optional on the 352 V-8 and larger engines.

Styling

Ford had now moved into a new era of styling at the Ford Design campus in Dearborn. George Walker, who had brought a vice president's title and much needed respect to Ford's design team during the 1950s, was now retired. Walker made it clear upon leaving that he wanted his longtime chief assistant,

Pricing for the 1962 Sunliner convertible started at $3,033.

1962 Ford Galaxie

The deep-dish steering wheel was meant to collapse under impact to prevent the driver from hitting the steering column. While not as effective as an airbag, it was progress in Ford's quest for safety.

Almost any engine was available in any full-size model Ford during the sixties. The 352 and 390 V-8 series were most popular among buyers.

Interiors were increasingly stylish, with rolled vinyl trim common in many models, whether bench seats or buckets.

Introduced in the 1950 sedans, the Ford crest was still prominently

Ford kept sales moving rapidly by introducing all-new body designs

Push-button AM radios became the standard on Galaxie models

Elwood Engle, to take over as head of Ford design. William Clay Ford, however, favored Gene Bordinat and appointed him as the new head of design. Upon hearing their decision, Engle accepted a position with Chrysler as head of their design studio. It had to have concerned Ford that Engle left with a thorough knowledge of all future Ford products.

Bordinat said he wasn't worried about Engle's move to Chrysler. "We really have no great concern about the security of our future products because of Elwood's switch to Chrysler. If nothing else, it would be a matter of pride for him or any other styling executive not to join another company just to report the secrets of his former company." However, Ford did recast its entire 1964 design lineup. "We have pretty thoroughly restyled our '64 cars, not for fear of Engle but for other reasons," said Bordinat. Ford had to protect itself and make sure the designs were not copied at Chrysler, and Bordinat moved quickly to obtain approval on fresh designs just in case.

When asked about the new direction of future Ford design, William Clay Ford said, "Primarily, we're getting more sensible, more feasible cars out of the advanced studio. We're not going so much for cars of the dream-car type. We want to be advanced, but we're keeping off 'cloud nine.'" With this new direction, Bordinat led four key stylists: Robert Maguire at the Advanced Studio, Joe Oros as head of the Ford Division Studio (and later, father of the Mustang design), Damon Woods as chief of the interior studios and A. B. Grisinger as head of the Lincoln-Mercury studios.

With these changes, Bordinat pushed for a more practical method of car design and produced many more full-size clay models, giving management a greater number of designs to choose from. He espoused the theory that a designer gets the "heebie geebies" three times with every car design. "Once just after it's too late to change the car, once just before it's introduced and once when they get the first 10-day (sales) report. It's like a woman and her baby," said Bordinat.

Galaxie

Galaxie was the name of the full-size game in 1962. Custom models were gone and Fairlane was now a mid-size. With three basic lines, Galaxie, Galaxie 500 and Galaxie 500XL, Ford still covered the basic, mid-range and luxury section its buyers wanted.

With 575,124 Galaxies produced in the 1962 model year, Ford knew where their profits came from. The new styling was still conservative although smooth and stylish. It came with a new mesh grille, no tail fins and all-new rear quarter panels with traditional Ford-style round tail lamps. Coolant changes were recommended every two years, and cars could go 30,000 miles between lubrication appointments. Oil changes were recommended every 6,000 miles.

The base Galaxie came in either Club or Town Sedan models. It provided 28 cubic feet of trunk space and a five-foot opening for easy luggage handling. Backseats

The 1960 Ford still provided the platform for the 1962 Galaxie family, but Ford stylists were busy bringing out an all-new look each year. The new Galaxie was much softer than the previous model and was gaining horsepower with each model year. (Photo: Ford Motor Company)

were spacious with plenty of headroom, and the base models were smooth riding although somewhat ill handling. Buyers were offered engines ranging from the standard Mileage Maker Six to the rubber-burning 406 cubic inch V-8.

Ford's Galaxie 500 models had upgraded chrome and trim levels and standard carpeted floors, a long list of luxury equipment and five optional vinyl interior packages. They were available in Club and Town Sedans, Club and Town Victoria hardtop models and a Sunliner convertible.

The Galaxie 500XL, introduced in February 1962, was the new top-of-the-line Ford. It came in either a hardtop coupe or Sunliner convertible with standard deep foam cushion bucket seats, a center console and all-vinyl seating surfaces. Sporty looking in either model, it came with a standard 292 V-8 or optional 352, 390 or 406 V-8 power plants.

If you needed the utility of a large wagon, Ford Galaxie had a spacious 93.5 cubic foot cargo space, a roll-down gate window and a quick fold-down rear seat.

These came in Ranch Wagon, Country Sedan and Country Squire models.

Ford accessories for 1962 included the PolarAire conditioner, a dealer-installed model capable of cooling, cleaning, dehumidifying and "depollenizing" the air in a new Ford. Brochures claimed it had the capacity to cool a four-room house. The SelectAire conditioner was the top-of-the-line choice, having a "five-room house" capacity and a three-speed blower, and also serving as a heater and defroster in cold weather.

Other popular accessories were backup lights, bumper guards, spotlights, remote rearview mirrors and power tailgate windows for wagons.

1962 Ford Options

385 hp 406 V-8	430.80
405 hp 406 V-8	488.70
Cruise-O-Matic	212.30
Overdrive	108.40
4-speed manual transmission	188.00
Power steering	81.70
4-way power seat	63.80
Power lift windows	102.10
SelectAire conditioner	360.90
Push-button radio	58.50

Fairlane

Ford saw opportunity in selling vehicles slotted between the highly successful Falcon and the strong-selling full-size Ford line. Having been working on the new mid-size format since 1959, Ford designers and engineers borrowed parts and pieces from the other models to keep costs down and developed a unique body style that still kept the Ford look. A new mid-size Fairlane was revealed on October 12, 1961, and was warmly received, selling more than 297,000 units in its first model year.

The mid-size Fairlane was just what Ford needed to fill out the dealer showrooms without cannibalizing the other models. It fit neatly between the Galaxie and Falcon and came standard with a 170 cubic inch, 101 hp six or an optional 221 V-8. The 260 cubic inch V-8 was offered with 164 hp late in the model year. Ford was still using the 2-speed Fordomatic transmission as the automatic option. The 221 V-8 was the only one offering a three-speed manual with overdrive.

Ford advertising boasted the new Fairlane had more interior space than the 1959 Ford and an overall length almost equal to the 1949 Ford. At 16 inches longer than the Falcon and 12 inches shorter than the Galaxie, Fairlane was designed to provide maximum driving comfort and utility with a minimum of maintenance.

Ford equipped the Fairlanes with 10-inch self-adjusting drum brakes. Just by applying the brakes while backing up, adjustments were completed. The front suspension was ball joint with top-mounted coil springs and sweptback control arms, similar to the big Fords.

The Fairlane 500 Sports Coupe, introduced on February 17, 1962, came with bucket seats

The Fairlane name was transferred from the full-size Ford family to the new mid-size model. Fairlane came with a standard I-6 engine or an optional 260 V-8 and saw 297,116 cars roll off the assembly line in the first year. (Photo: Ford Motor Company)

patterned after the Thunderbird seats and a center console with a compartment for storing personal items.

1962 Fairlane Options

Fordomatic	189.60
Push-button radio	58.50
Power steering	81.70
Power brakes	43.20
164 hp 260 Challenger V-8	103.00
Front seat belts	16.80
Padded dash & visors	24.30
Two-tone paint	22.00
PolarAire conditioner	270.90
Overdrive	108.40

Falcon

Ford was extremely happy with the success of its Falcon compact. The body styling for 1962 was still only a mild facelift but at the Chicago Auto Show, the Futura Sports coupe was introduced with a fully synchronized four-speed manual transmission and the standard 170 cubic inch I-6 engine. It had unique exterior chrome trim; chrome wheel covers; and Thunderbird-like roof, seats and center console. Ford also offered an optional vinyl roof in either black or white.

Striving to personalize the sales brochures for Falcon, Ford quoted actual owners on everything from performance to economy. In one dealer handout Ford supported its claim of 30 mpg on the standard 144 cubic inch six. "We have checked time after time and we get 30.4 miles to the gallon," said Mr. and Mrs. C. Lund, of Hutchinson, Minnesota. Similar quotes from Ford buyers supporting Ford's bragging points sounded less like the company tooting its own horn.

Ford was using Zinclad-coated rocker panels and main underbody structure pieces to slow down the rusting process. Ford advertised its double-wrapped, aluminized mufflers

as having three times the normal life. The Diamond Lustre paint, according to Ford, "never needs waxing." All of this was part of a continuing effort to show how inexpensive upkeep could be on a Ford.

Safety equipment on Falcon included the deep-dish steering wheel, Double-Grip door locks, optional seat belts, and padded dash and sun visors.

Single-unit body construction was used for Falcon and Fairlane, cutting down on squeaks and rattles while providing a stronger overall structure.

1962 Falcon Options

Falcon 170 Special I-6	37.40
Fordomatic	163.10
Push-button radio	58.50
Front seat belts	20.60
Padded dash & visors	21.80
Windshield washer	13.70
Whitewall tires	29.90
Two-speed electric wipers	9.65
Backup lights	10.70

The Falcon Sedan Delivery was ideal for small businesses making light cargo deliveries. It was easy on gas, simple to drive and affordable.

Falcon Sports Futura was introduced at the Chicago Auto Show on February 17, 1962. It was available with a floor-mounted four-speed transmission and a 101 horsepower 170 I-6 engine. (Photos this page: Ford Motor Company)

The soft top could operate with the Roadster fiberglass unit in place.

Coming standard with Kelsey-Hayes wire wheels, the Thunderbird Roadster package brought the 'Bird to $5,439, a steep price for 1962.

The Thunderbird Roadster option package sacrificed practicality for style, taking up most of the usable luggage space. (Photos this page: Ford Motor Company)

Thunderbird

Thunderbird Sports Roadster and Landau models were introduced to add some life to the otherwise unchanged body styles. The 300 horsepower 390 cubic inch V-8 was carried over for 1962, and all-new models came standard with a swing-away steering wheel, allowing the driver to enter and exit the Thunderbird more easily than traditional vehicles.

The Sports Roadster model essentially allowed Ford to add some inexpensive pizzazz to the lineup. By adding a fiberglass shell that fit neatly over the rear seating area, the Thunderbird was transformed into a two-seater sports luxury car. The Thunderbirds all required premium fuel and the $5,439 Sports Roadster could manage zero-to-60 mph in 9.7 seconds. Its top speed as tested by *Mechanix Illustrated* magazine was 115 mph at the Daytona Speedway.

The Sports package also included Kelsey-Hayes wire wheels with simulated knockoff hubs that looked great and were quite popular until Elvis Presley reported a collapsed wheel on his Roadster. That prompted Ford to recall the cars and recheck the adjustable wire spokes. Many were replaced with solid wheels.

The Roadster also included a special gull-wing bird emblem over a red, white and blue crest mounted on the front fenders below the Thunderbird script and on the tonneau cover.

The Landau was an even less expensive model to produce, as it really had nothing more than a vinyl roof and minor trim changes. The roof came in either black or white only and had chrome Landau bars on the C-pillars.

Thunderbird rear quarter panels had three new chrome bars to replace the 1961's four chrome strips. The grille was changed to a square-block style. The doors now opened a full four feet, allowing passengers easy entry or exit and possibly causing body damage to the car parked next to it. Temperature and air conditioning controls were all moved to the center console. The taillights now combined stoplights, brake lights and parking lights as one unit.

Lee Iacocca commented that the "totally new engineering features make the 1962 Thunderbird the most advanced, yet most practical, car in the industry."

1962 Thunderbird Options

340 hp 390 V-8	242.10
SelectAire conditioning	415.10
Power windows	106.20
4-way power seat	92.10
Console Range radio	112.80
Two-tone paint	25.80
Tinted glass	43.00
Front seat belts	22.80
Leather seat inserts	106.20

Cobra

Shortly after winning Le Mans in 1959, star American driver Carroll Shelby had been diagnosed with heart problems that took him out of the cockpit and into car manufacturing. "I built three Corvettes," said Shelby, "and I sold one to Jim Hall, one to Gary Laughlin and one to a doctor in Houston. I was building them and Ed Cole [of Chevrolet] called me and said, 'Shelby, I don't want to have anything to do with that project.'" Cole apparently had received word that official support for racing was coming to an end and there would be no more association with Shelby.

Carroll Shelby next began working on an idea he had to mate a Ford Challenger 260 V-8 with an aluminum-bodied English AC roadster chassis. "I never went to anybody but Ford on the AC," said Shelby. AC Cars of Thames was losing its source for an engine and saw the Shelby offer as a way to keep producing the graceful little sports car.

Shelby moved from his home state of Texas to Southern California to start the project. The first two cars were built in friend Dean Moon's shop. "I was focused on Ford because they came out with a new engine and they didn't have a sports car," said Shelby. "So I went to Iacocca and said, 'I'll build you a new sports car if you give me a little money.' He always looked at the big picture but he depended on Don Frey [chief Ford engineer] to do it." Taking about a day to install the running gear in their first AC, Shelby and Moon drove the first Cobra out of the shop and found acceleration in the lightweight roadster exhilarating.

Although the first Shelby Cobra rolled out of Dean Moon's race shop in Los Angeles in February 1962, most of the year was spent in development leading up to full production by 1963. Shelby worked diligently to get his vehicle certified by the Federation Internationale de L'Automobile (FIA) as a GT III car, which would allow him to pit the Cobra against Ferrari and other key racing names in international competition during the 1963 season. High-visibility events like Le Mans were important to the effort. He promoted the new sports cars to the press, painting the same vehicle a different color for each road test to leave the impression that he had a whole fleet on the ground.

By March 1962, Shelby had expanded to a new facility in Venice, California, becoming Shelby American, as Ford agreed to become involved. Ford finance man Ray Geddes set up an office at the facility to coordinate the Shelby-Ford effort.

According to Shelby, he came up with the name "Cobra" in a dream. "I woke up and jotted the name down on a pad which I kept by my bedside and went back to sleep." He said the next morning when he woke up and saw the Cobra name written down, he knew it was right and stuck with it. To this day hearing his Cobra referred to as an AC Cobra still irritates Shelby. "There was never an 'AC Cobra.' The name was 'Shelby' with a little bitty 'ac' there and then 'Cobra.'" Shelby and Ford put together a network of special dealers that could sell the hot little aluminum rocket. The Cobra was Shelby's baby, and the legend began.

Concepts

In late 1962 Ford started showing off the Mustang concept sports car, even taking it on tour in 1963. Really more of a competition concept for Ford than a

Ford Engines for 1962

CID	Carb.	Comp.	HP
144 I-6	1 bbl	8.7	85 @ 4200
170 I-6	1 bbl	8.7	101 @ 4400
223 I-6	1 bbl	8.4	138 @ 4200
221 V-8	2 bbl	8.7	145 @ 4400
260 V-8	2 bbl	8.7	164 @ 4400
292 V-8	2 bbl	8.8	170 @ 4200
352 V-8	2 bbl	8.9	220 @ 4400
390 V-8	4 bbl	9.6	300 @ 4600
390 V-8	3x2 bbl	10.5	340 @ 5000
390 V-8	4 bbl	10.6	375 @ 6000
390 V-8	3x2 bbl	11.1	401 @ 6000
406 V-8	4 bbl	10.9	385 @ 5800
406 V-8	3x2 bbl	10.9	405 @ 5800

The Ford Cougar 406 was a drivable concept and was first shown to the public on February 17 at the Chicago Auto Show. The 49.5-inch-high vehicle had electrically operated gull-wing doors.

The Cougar, which actually started life as a 1954 concept design, was brought to life in 1962 with a 406 V-8 under the hood. (Photos this page: Ford Motor Company)

predecessor to the 1964½ Mustang production car, it was first shown running a pre-race lap at the U.S. Grand Prix at Watkins Glen, New York, on October 7, 1962. Powered by a 106 horsepower V-4 engine developed by Ford of Germany, the Mustang was capable of 117 mph. It was designed by Ford stylists to compete with European

sports cars and could attain 35 mpg. The mid-engine sports car was only 28.8 inches high at the hood and 39.4 inches at the top of the roll bar. The 1,500 pound car incorporated pop-up headlamps pivoting 180 degrees at night. The body was made of aluminum, and the steering wheel and foot pedals were adjustable to fit the driver.

Ford would often recycle concept cars by freshening them up and shipping them off to the show circuit again. The Cougar 406 show car, based on an earlier mid–1950s design called the D-523, was brought back to life in 1962. Ford designers removed the fender skirts, dropped in a hot 406 V-8 engine and mounted Kelsey-

Hayes wire wheels. It was built on a modified 1955 Thunderbird chassis, originally powered by a 312 cubic inch V-8. The show car had a fully padded wraparound dash, a center console with a floor-mounted shifter and a telescoping steering wheel.

Another innovative design first shown in 1962 at the Seattle World's Fair was the ⅜th scale Seattle-ite XXI—a six-wheel show model with fins and rocket-like afterburner taillights. The tandem front wheels all steered and the designers envisioned it having a travel programming computer, interchangeable power packages, variable density glass to keep the interior cool and fingertip steering. Although never built to full scale, the Seattle-ite drew enthusiastic crowds during the fair.

It appeared that with Gene Bordinat at the design helm, these far-out models would soon disappear in favor of more conservative concepts that would dovetail better with the Advanced Engineering Department's plans. While not as exciting as past dream cars, concept vehicles under Bordinat's leadership would have more of a chance to see actual production.

The Cougar 406 interior featured wraparound padding that covered the face of the dash and melded into the armrests and console. Cougar had roll-up windows, had a floor-mounted shift, and was fully functional.

1962 Model Car Pricing

Falcon
Fordor Sedan	$2,047
Tudor Sedan	$1,985
Futura Coupe	$2,232
Fordor Deluxe Wagon	$2,427
Squire Wagon	$2,603

Fairlane
4-door I-6	$2,216
4-door V-8	$2,319

Fairlane 500
2-door Sports Coupe I-6	$2,504
2-door Sports Coupe V-8	$2,607

Galaxie
2-door Galaxie Club Sedan	$2,507
4-door Galaxie Town Sedan	$2,616

Galaxie 500
Town Victoria 4-door I-6	$2,739
Club Victoria V-8	$2,783
Sunliner Convertible V-8	$3,033

Galaxie 500XL
Club Victoria V-8	$3,106
Convertible	$3,358

Station Wagons
Ranch Wagon 6-passenger I-6	$2,733
Country Squire 9-passenger I-6	$3,088
Country Squire 9-passenger V-8	$3,197

Thunderbird
Coupe	$4,321
Landau	$4,398
Convertible	$4,788
Convertible Roadster Package	$5,439

The Seattle-ite XXI concept car was actually a ⅜th scale model created by the Ford design studio. The tandem-mounted front-drive wheels and travel programming computer never saw a city street and were intended to inspire auto show attendees. (Photos this page: Ford Motor Company)

The Mustang started life as a concept car to test the public's reaction. Ford wanted something lightweight, sporty, affordable and performance oriented.

Mustang I came with pop-up headlamps, bucket seats, a midship V-4 engine and two rear-mounted radiators.

The concept car was in auto shows and was taken on a tour across the country to drum up positive feedback from buyers. However, Ford had no intention of building a Mustang quite this unconventional. "Tease them with a sports car, but give them what they'll buy" was Ford's approach. (Photos this page: Ford Motor Company)

1962 Car Production

Fairlane	
4-door Sedan	45,342
2-door Sedan	34,264
Fairlane 500	
4-door Sedan	129,258
2-door Sedan	68,624
2-door Sedan, Bucket Seats	19,628
Falcon	
Fordor Sedan	126,041
Tudor Sedan	143,650
2-door Sedan, Sports Futura	17,011
Fordor Wagon	66,819
4-door Squire Wagon	22,583
Tudor Wagon	20,025
Sedan Delivery	1,568
Ranchero	20,842
Galaxie	
4-door Sedan	115,594
2-door Sedan	54,930
Galaxie 500	
4-door Sedan	174,195
2-door Sedan	27,824
4-door Hardtop	30,778
2-door Hardtop	87,562
2-door Hardtop, Bucket Seats	28,412
Convertible	42,646
Convertible, Bucket Seats	13,183
Station Wagons	
4-door City Sedan 6-passenger	47,635
4-door City Sedan 9-passenger	16,562
4-door City Squire 6-passenger	16,114
4-door City Squire 9-passenger	15,666
4-door Ranch Wagon 6-passenger	33,674
Business Club Wagon	18,153
Thunderbird	
2-door Hardtop	68,127
Convertible	9,884
Total	**1,516,594**

▶

By 1963 Carroll Shelby's Ford Cobra Roadster was making a splash in the sports car world and setting records on the track.

FORD

The Year 1963

In its second year of the rocket design, Thunderbird still offered lots of style and was the first vehicle to come standard with retractable front safety lap belts.

Nineteen sixty-three was Ford's most successful model year in its 60-year history, setting new records in worldwide factory sales, dollar sales, earnings, employment and employee payrolls. This success was due to a good economy, exciting new products and talented management. Henry II's support of Ford's worldwide involvement in racing events placed the Ford brand in the news often, and times were good.

Worldwide sales were up more than 9 percent and net income for 1963 was U.S. $488.5 million. Non-U.S. sales were up an amazing 22.5 percent over the previous year. Even employment was up, with 316,568 men and women working for the company and a payroll of more than $1.9 billion. The company was continuing to spend more each year to build new plants and update others, putting the pressure on cross-town rival Chevrolet to keep up with investment, sales and new products.

The company's biggest challenge was to continue turning record profits. Since 1959, Ford had charged only minor price increases on its products. With labor costs going up 23 percent, it was becoming increasingly tough to keep the profits at high levels.

Moving into 1963 Ford was on top of its game, with some of the all-time great engines and body designs coming out of Dearborn. The company had great products and changes coming out just about every six months, keeping pressure on the competition.

This was the year of the car enthusiast. Ford marketing started the "Total Performance" theme for its advertising campaigns, referring to automobiles that performed in road ability, braking power, steering performance and visibility. And if the Ford line of engines was any indication, rubber burning was a part of the Total Performance program as well.

Ford opened the model year once again with a new Galaxie body design. Falcon was still using the same body, although now trimmed with more chrome, new wheels and sportier options. Thunderbird was mostly a carry-over and in its last year for the existing body style. Fairlane was coming quickly into the sporty world with a 260 V-8, bucket seats and four-on-the-floor, and would soon start seeing competition on the drag strips. Another major piece of Ford performance hit the asphalt that year in the form of the AC-bodied Shelby Cobra. The first models, built with a 260 V-8, caused quite a stir in the automotive world. And no one realized just yet what venom it packed.

Galaxie

Ford's bread-and-butter vehicle was the Galaxie lineup. This year Ford brought a base model back into the mix with the Ford 300, comparable to the earlier Custom series, sold mostly to businesses and fleets. A total of 755,140 of the various full-size Galaxie models were built in 1963, accounting for more than half of all Ford car production and giving the company's management a good idea where profits were coming from. With new models and engines coming in both the fall and spring, 1963 was an exciting time for Ford enthusiasts.

1963 Ford Options

405 hp 406 V-8	391.30
425 hp 427 V-8	570.60
Fordomatic	189.60
Cruise-O-Matic	212.30
SelectAire conditioning	360.90
Power steering	81.70
Power brakes	43.20
Power windows	102.10
Windshield washer	20.10
Two-tone paint	22.00

Styling for 1963 again changed dramatically, featuring large, round taillights, no fins and a concave front grille. Ford had a dual purpose in mind when it brought out a new 500XL Fastback model in January. First, it kept a dizzying array of new models coming, and second, it made certain that the new Fastback roofline qualified for NASCAR events as a production model.

The convertible-like hardtop with narrow B-pillars was more aerodynamic than the boxy T-Bird–style roof on the other models and helped the Fords cut through the air at the super speedways. The designers had little trouble making the new, smoother Galaxie models run well, powered by the all-new 427 cubic inch V-8. Led by Tiny Lund, Fords swept the first five positions at the Daytona 500, stunning General Motors and Chrysler teams in the February event. They proceeded to dominate almost every super speedway event that year.

More Thunderbird features began easing their way into the Galaxie lineup. Top-of-the-line models came with bucket seats and a console, and a swing-away steering column was an extra-cost option.

The two 427 V-8 power plants made big news as the most powerful production engines ever offered by Ford. The 427 probably ranks high on the top ten list of all-time performance engines. The single four-barrel version produced 410 horsepower at 5,600 rpm, and the dual four-barrel model pumped out 425 horsepower at 6,000 rpm. The big engines were available in all full-size Fords except the wagons.

You could order your hot rod with the Synchro-Smooth three-speed manual, a four-speed floor-mounted manual or an automatic transmission.

Ford's Club Victoria Galaxie model utilized the T-Bird–style roofline. Ford produced 29,713 of the hardtop models.

The 1963 Galaxie convertible is still one of the most collected Ford ragtops. Afterburner tail lamps and hot engine offerings gave it the sporting image Ford was looking for. (Photos this page: Ford Motor Company)

1963 Galaxie 500

Galaxie, Galaxie 500 and Galaxie 500XL models covered the total full-size Ford offerings for 1963. Galaxie received another all-new body design, and within four months of its introduction, Ford announced the racing-inspired 1963½ Fastback models.

The large, round tail lamps were inspired by Thunderbird but lacked the fins.

Filling the tank was handled at the rear of the vehicle. The filler was hidden behind a drop-down panel similar to

Trunk space continued to be large enough to accommodate the entire

1963 Futura Sprint Fastback

Futura Sprint, with a 260 V-8 engine, could manage zero-to-60 mph in around 12 seconds. But keep in mind that a four-speed 170 six-cylinder took more than 19 seconds to get there!

Another important power addition to the big Ford lineup was the 289 cubic inch V-8. This replacement for the older 292 V-8 produced more power, 195 horsepower at 4,400 rpm, and got better mileage—all on regular gas.

Falcon

Falcon, while carrying the basic body style for one more year, picked up new hardtop and convertible models. The Futura convertible model could be ordered with bench or bucket seats and came with a power-operated ragtop. The top was anchored to each individual roof bow to prevent "ballooning" at speed. Standard were pleated all-vinyl bench seats. Bucket seats and a center console were extra-cost options.

Standard power for the Futura convertible was a 170 cubic inch six cylinder producing 101 horsepower. The 260 V-8 option was introduced later in the model year and offered snappy performance the underpowered six couldn't match.

In a *Motor Trend* road test, the six-cylinder Falcon convertible equipped with a four-speed transmission could only muster zero-to-60 mph in 19.6 seconds. Writer Jim Wright said, "The absolute top speed with this particular car was 90 mph, and that took quite a long time." The fuel economy figures showed a high of 23.7 mpg under highway cruising. The brakes apparently were adequate on the 2,754-pound vehicle, bringing the car to repeated straight-line stops from 60 mph. "We used the brakes hard during all the acceleration and top-speed runs, but didn't notice any excessive fade or pedal pressure build-up," Wright continued.

The new Falcon Sprint series, introduced in January 1963 as a 1963½ model, came standard with the new 260 Challenger

Falcon offered its first convertible in 1963, adding more sporty choices for enthusiastic buyers. The base-model sedan was still listed at a comfortable $1,985. (Photo: Ford Motor Company)

V-8 producing 164 horsepower at 4,400 rpm, making the lightweight Falcon come alive. In dealer showrooms by February 22, the Sprint came in convertible form or the new Fastback hardtop, giving it the look of its 1963½ big brother, Galaxie. Ordering the Sprint automatically gave you a 260 V-8, four-speed manual transmission, tachometer and chrome air cleaner, valve covers, radiator cap and dipstick. All other model Falcons except for the Futura convertible came standard with the 144 cubic inch 85 horsepower six cylinder, although the hardtops almost always came with the 170 cubic inch six. Customers who ordered a six cylinder with an automatic received a 200 cubic inch engine developing 116 horsepower. The Challenger 260 engine was available with all Falcon models at extra cost.

1963 Falcon Options

Fordomatic	172.90
Push-button radio	58.50
Power steering	81.70
Padded dash & visors	21.80
4-speed transmission	188.00
Tinted windshield	12.95
Luggage rack	45.40
Backup lights	10.70
Challenger 260 engine	196.30

Thunderbird

Ford promoted the new Thunderbird as having "2,500 engineering and design modifications." Iacocca was quoted as saying, "Thunderbird is the most changed car we are offering for 1963." The exterior showed little visible change and while most people probably didn't see it as the "most changed" of the Ford models, it did incorporate many refinements.

Ford added 150 pounds of sound deadener to decrease wind noise, modified the exhaust pipes, and added two-inch longer wiper blades and a hydraulic wiper motor.

Thunderbird could now go 100,000 miles between lubrication services. Standard on the Thunderbird was a dual-range automatic transmission, power steering and brakes, swing-away steering column, backup lights and wheel covers. Undercoating and remote-control mirrors were also included in the base price of $4,445.

For 1963, Thunderbird still came with a 300 horsepower 390 V-8 and now there was an optional 340 horsepower 390 V-8 for those needing the occasional adrenaline rush. The optional 390 V-8 had 10.5:1 compression and found its peak horsepower at 5,000 rpm.

Thunderbird sales dropped to 63,313, almost 15,000 units less than the prior year. So this would be the last season for the rocket design before a changeover to the really big bodies that would take the thunder out of the 'Bird.

1963 Thunderbird Options

SelectAire conditioning	415.10
Power windows	106.20
4-way power seat	92.10
Leather seat inserts	106.20
Two-tone paint	25.80
Wire wheels	373.30

Fairlane

Fairlane was now in its second year and doing well. Sales were up by more than 50,000 units over 1962, and it provided healthy profits for the company and an opportunity to bring new buyers into their first Ford. Fairlane continued to stay well ahead of Chevy II in sales.

The Fairlanes rolled into dealerships on September 28, 1962, with a new Fairlane 500 hardtop and a series of station wagons. The sports coupe model was now based on the hardtop body style, not the sedan, and still featured bucket seats and a full-length console.

While the 170 cubic inch six was standard, the Fairlanes could be optioned up to the 260 Challenger V-8 or the new 289 V-8 with a four-barrel producing 271 horsepower at 6,000 rpm. The 289 V-8 was a late introduction and available only on sedans and hardtops—not on wagons. Both V-8s could be ordered with a four-speed manual transmission.

This would also be the first year for an all-synchronized three-speed manual column-mounted shifter. By mid-year all Fairlanes equipped with Fordomatic came standard with the 200 cubic inch six engine.

1963 Model Car Pricing

Falcon

2-door Sedan	$1,985
Futura 4-door Sedan	$2,165
Futura 2-door Sports Hardtop	$2,319
Futura Convertible	$2,591
Sprint 2-door Hardtop V-8	$2,603
Sprint Convertible V-8	$2,837

Fairlane

4-door Sedan I-6	$2,216
4-door Sedan V-8	$2,319

Fairlane 500

2-door Sedan I-6	$2,242
4-door Sedan I-6	$2,304
Sports Coupe I-6	$2,504

Fairlane Wagons

Ranch Wagon I-6	$2,525
Custom Ranch Wagon I-6	$2,613
Fairlane Squire Wagon I-6	$2,781

Galaxie

2-door Sedan I-6	$2,453
4-door Sedan I-6	$2,507

Galaxie 500

2-door Hardtop I-6	$2,674
4-door Hardtop I-6	$2,739
Convertible I-6	$2,924

Galaxie 500XL

2-door Hardtop V-8	$3,268
4-door Hardtop V-8	$3,333
Convertible	$3,518

Station Wagons

Country Sedan I-6	$2,933
Country Squire I-6	$3,018

Thunderbird

Coupe	$4,445
Landau	$4,548
Convertible	$4,912
Convertible Roadster Package	$5,563

1963 Futura Sprint Fastback

The Futura Sprint Fastback became available in January 1963 and was an overnight success. You could have an automatic transmission for $173 and power steering for $82.

The Sprint came standard with the Challenger 260 V-8 producing 164 horsepower.

Sprint's bucket seats were standard, as were self-adjusting brakes. For the 1963 model year, Ford produced close to 350,000 Falcons including the

The Sprint insignia on the front fenders told other Falcon owners you

1963 Futura Sprint Fastback

The 1963 Falcon Futura Sprint V-8 Fastback was in dealer showrooms on February 22. At $2,603 it came with a four-speed transmission, bucket seats, tachometer and a racing-like steering wheel.

The Sports Roadster option was in its second year, and while not a big part of production, Ford often used it in print advertising to create a stylish image for the T-Bird.

The 1963 Thunderbird Laudau model could be spotted by its vinyl roof and the chrome Laudau Bars on the C-pillars. (Photo: Ford Motor Company)

The Fairlane Squire was the top-of-the-line wagon, with the Ford traditional simulated wood grain and moldings on the side panels. Bucket seats were optional in the Squire, and full carpeting and a power tailgate window were standard. With rear seats in a fold-down position, the Fairlane wagon had 49.3 cubic feet of cargo space and an extra five cubic feet of storage below the floor level. It had a full eight feet of space end to end and almost five feet side to side.

1963 Fairlane Options

271 hp 289 V-8	424.80
Fordomatic	189.60
Push-button radio	58.50
Power steering	81.70
Power brakes	43.20
Front seat belts	16.80
4-speed transmission	188.00

Thunderbird's interior featured foam-cushioned bucket seats, the now traditional T-Bird console and pleated fabric upholstery.

Thunderbird featured a swing-away steering wheel and deep-set gauges to reduce sun glare.

A 390 V-8 with 300 horsepower was standard, with an available 340 horsepower version offered.

The designers moved the three

Thunderbird received a new

The afterburner-style tail lamps

1963 Thunderbird Convertible

Thunderbird designers moved the trim around, changed the grille, and moved the "Thunderbird" signature to the rear fenders. (Photos this page: Ford Motor Company)

A standard power top used a mechanism similar to that in the 1957–59 Ford Skyliner model hardtop convertibles.

Full instrumentation, bucket seats and room for four were standard in Thunderbird.

Although all Thunderbirds came with a 300 horsepower 390 V-8, an optional 340 horse version with three

The original Shelby Cobra came with an array of gauges and a polished walnut steering wheel.

The Cobra was $5,995 when it went on sale in 1963. Shelby originally targeted Ford because they had just introduced the new Challenger engine and didn't have a sports car in their lineup.

Cobra

Ford needed a quick way to include a sports car in their lineup—something that would compete with Corvette's new Sting Ray. Carroll Shelby's company, Shelby American, had come around at just the right time to fill that need. His Cobra fit the bill, and by January 1963 the roadsters were starting to make big waves on the streets and on racetracks. Ford Division produced a heavy advertising campaign based around Total Performance and included Shelby's lightweight Cobra roadsters in its materials.

An article in the *Ford Today* publication said, "For his scorching Cobra, Shelby chose to mate an excellent-handling British sports car with a reliable and powerful American engine. With virtually any power plant available to him, but with proven reliability and parts availability factors of prime concern, Shelby chose Ford's 260 cubic inch Challenger." Shelby had upped the Challenger's horsepower to 260 and added a four-speed from a Galaxie 406. Ford made a point of comparing the Cobra directly to the all-new Corvette Sting Ray. One of the better known reprints in the Ford literature was

from a *San Francisco Chronicle* article titled "Shocking News." The article said, "Shocking news from Riverside was the complete annihilation of the highly respected Corvette Sting Rays by a pair of Ford-powered Cobras in the races for big production cars." It described the Sting Ray drivers as shell-shocked. "The Cobras ate them alive, turning times five to eight seconds a lap faster time than the Sting Rays. In the hands of El Monte's Dave MacDonald and Ken Miles, the Cobras were faster on the straights and out-cornered and out-braked the Corvettes."

Ford Engines for 1963			
CID	Carb.	Comp.	HP
144 I-6	1 bbl	8.7	85 @ 4200
170 I-6	1 bbl	8.7	101 @ 4400
200 I-6	1 bbl	8.7	116 @ 4400
223 I-6	1 bbl	8.4	138 @ 4200
221 V-8	2 bbl	8.7	145 @ 4400
260 V-8	2 bbl	8.7	164 @ 4400
289 V-8	2 bbl	8.7	195 @ 4400
289 V-8	4 bbl	9.0	210 @ 4400
289 V-8	4 bbl	10.5	271 @ 6000
352 V-8	2 bbl	8.9	220 @ 4400
390 V-8	4 bbl	9.6	300 @ 4600
390 V-8	3x2 bbl	10.5	340 @ 5000
406 V-8	4 bbl	11.4	385 @ 5800
406 V-8	3x2 bbl	12.1	405 @ 5800
427 V-8	4 bbl	11.6	410 @ 5600
427 V-8	2x4 bbl	12.0	425 @ 6000

1963 Cobra 289

1963 Cobra 289

For a Corvette owner, there was really nothing about the Cobra's appearance that would indicate its bite was lethal.

Golf clubs and Cobras weren't meant to go together—unless you wanted to strap the bag into the passenger seat. The trunk was meant for a tire and perhaps a sandwich.

The 289 Shelby Cobras came equipped with aircraft lap belts and small bucket seats. The wraparound backs kept you in place under hard cornering.

The very first models used Ford's 260 Challenger V-8. In a Motor Trend road test, the Cobra 289 clocked a zero-to-60 mph time of 5.8 seconds. The testers said it could have made it in 5 seconds flat with bigger tires.

1963 Car Production

Falcon

Standard 4-door Sedan	62,365
Standard 2-door Sedan	70,630
Standard Convertible	18,942
Futura 4-door Sedan	31,736
Futura 2-door Sedan	16,674
Futura 2-door Sedan, Bucket Seats	10,344
Futura 2-door Hardtop	17,524
Futura 2-door Hardtop, Bucket Seats	10,972
Futura Convertible	12,250
Sprint 2-door Hardtop	10,479
Sprint Convertible	4,602

Falcon Wagons

2-door Wagon Standard	7,322
4-door Wagon Standard	18,484
2-door Wagon Deluxe	4,269
4-door Wagon Deluxe	23,477
4-door Squire	6,808
4-door Squire Deluxe	1,461

Falcon Sedan Delivery

2-door Standard	925
2-door Deluxe	113

Falcon Ranchero

2-door Standard	12,218
2-door Deluxe	6,315

Fairlane

4-door Sedan	44,454
2-door Sedan	28,984
4-door Wagon	24,006

Fairlane 500

4-door Sedan	104,175
2-door Sedan	34,764
2-door Hardtop	41,641
2-door Hardtop, Bucket Seats	28,268

2-door Wagon	29,612
4-door Squire Wagon	7,706
4-door Squire Wagon, Bucket Seats	277

Ford 300

4-door Sedan	44,142
2-door Sedan	26,010

Galaxie

4-door Sedan	82,419
2-door Sedan	30,335

Galaxie 500

4-door Sedan	205,722
2-door Sedan	21,137
4-door Hardtop	26,558
4-door Hardtop, Bucket Seats	12,596
2-door Hardtop Fastback	100,500
2-door Hardtop Fastback, Bucket Seats	33,870
2-door Hardtop	49,733
2-door Hardtop, Bucket Seats	29,713
Convertible	36,876
Convertible, Bucket Seats	18,551

Galaxie Wagons (4-door)

Country Squire 9-passenger	19,246
Country Sedan 6-passenger	64,954
Country Sedan 9-passenger	22,250
Country Squire, 6-passenger, Bucket Seats	437
Country Squire 6-passenger	19,922
Country Squire, 9-passenger, Bucket Seats	321

Thunderbird

2-door Hardtop	42,806
2-door Landau	14,139
2-door Convertible	5,913
2-door Roadster	455
Total	**1,600,402**

This was just the sort of promotion Ford was looking for from the press.

The initial roadsters came with the Challenger 260 V-8 with 10:1 compression. Producing one horsepower per cubic inch, the engine almost put too much stress on the AC chassis. Being built on a chassis that was meant to handle a four-cylinder engine, the vehicle needed extra strength to accommodate a V-8. All the torque and horsepower added up to popped rivets, loose nuts and bolts, and squeaks and rattles. Knowing that Ford dealers were signing up to move his metal, Shelby's crew made numerous changes and added the new 289 V-8 to all Cobras rolling out the door. He also updated the latest

Cobras by replacing the original Lucas wiring harnesses with Ford materials and the Smith gauges with Stewart-Warner units.

The Cobra was receiving good reports from the automotive press, which loved the performance. Tom McCahill, writing for *Mechanix Illustrated*, said the 260 V-8 typically produced zero-to-60 times in the five-second range—or lower if you believed the Shelby headquarters, which boasted 4.1 seconds. Most of the writers complained that getting power to the ground was the main problem; however, there wasn't much room for fitting bigger tires under the existing fenders. McCahill summed up the Cobra's acceleration in a one-liner: "It is a real hairy-chested, swashbuckling little rat that will snap Gramps' head right off his shoulders if you hit the go pedal when he isn't ready." He said the thing that impressed him most about the Cobra, after getting past the handling and performance, was its solid feel. Cobra roadster production was evolutionary, with Shelby American making many changes and improvements as they went along. Their racing versions were often used as a guide for what would need changing on the street models. The ultra stress of a six-hour race was like putting 100,000 miles on a street vehicle, telling them what parts would fail and what would need reinforcing.

With plenty of speed and snappy handling, the Cobra was quickly gaining a reputation as the quickest production car around. And for $5,995 it was a bargain, even in 1963.

▶

Even though the Mustang was designed and marketed by a team, it was Iacocca who brought the idea to life. His Mustang was one of the most successful models in Ford history and provided the company with substantial profits for decades to come.

With only the front end disguised, Mustang II concept was put out on the show circuit shortly before the release of the Mustang to build excitement. (Photo: Ford Motor Company)

FORD

The Year 1964

The first Mustang rolled off the assembly line on March 9, 1964. More than $3.5 million was invested in the Dearborn Rouge Plant prior to production of the new sports coupe, which was built on the same line as the Fairlane sedans.

Henry Ford II told his investors at the annual stockholders' meeting on February 12, 1964, that they should visit the Ford Pavilion at the New York World's Fair, opening on April 22. He chatted about the Magic Skyway display, designed by Walt Disney, and then he gave the audience the first clue of things to come.

"One highlight of the Ford product display deserves special mention—an all-new car named the Mustang. Production of the Mustang is scheduled to begin in March at Dearborn, and full details about the car will be made public in mid-April. We invite all stockholders to visit the Ford exhibit." Little did the audience know what the new car would do for their stock portfolios.

Henry Ford II continued as chairman of the board, and the president was Arjay Miller. Henry's younger brothers Benson and William Clay were also on the board, along with former chairman Ernie Breech and former president John Dykstra.

Business was still good and Total Performance continued to be the advertising theme. Ford picked up the *Motor Trend* Car of the Year Award for the total 1964 lineup, a rather unusual format for the magazine's award. Receiving the award for a complete lineup had happened only once before,

when Ford won for their safety efforts in 1956.

For a third consecutive year Ford posted record sales and earnings despite more localized union strikes. Ford worldwide sales were up 10.6 percent to U.S. $9.6 billion with a net income of only $505 million. Henry pointed out to investors that Ford's costs were still climbing, and there were substantial increases in the areas of labor and product improvements while sticker prices on new cars remained even. This brought the actual return on invested dollars down from 5.7 percent to 5.3 percent in 1964. The company also spent $463 million during 1964 to expand production capacity at its plants around the world.

Ford Motor Company sold just under four million cars and trucks in 1964 worldwide and more than 2.6 million of those were sold in the United States.

Ford now had operations in 21 countries around the world. Non-U.S. business had grown more than 50 percent since 1959, accounting for about one-third of Ford's total vehicle sales.

Galaxie

Ford's 1964 Galaxie lineup kept pace with another new body design and interior, while the power train and mechanicals were mildly upgraded. Everything new seemed to be attributed to the Total Performance theme, including the life-of-the-car transmission fluid, aluminized mufflers, 6,000-mile oil changes, and the extensive body corrosion protection.

Engines continued to range from the standard six-cylinder all the way up to the 425 horsepower 427 V-8. The Galaxie 500XL models came standard with the 289 V-8 while all others came with the six.

Convertible models now came with a tempered glass rear window, replacing the plastic versions that crinkled and yellowed with age. The boot cover was improved by using a stretch vinyl that more easily snapped in place and gave a wrinkle-free appearance. The top used an electrically powered hydraulic system for raising or lowering. The four-door hardtops featured a

1964 Timeline
- Mustang is introduced April 17
- Introduced: Kennedy half-dollar, Diet Pepsi and Maxim freeze-dried coffee
- Go-go girls dance to the frug, swim, watusi and monkey
- The Beatles get $2,400 for their first Ed Sullivan appearance
- Cigarette packs carry first Surgeon General warnings
- Best Picture Oscar: *My Fair Lady* starring Rex Harrison

Service intervals were increased with Ford's life-of-the-car transmission fluid and rear-axle lubricant, aluminized mufflers and 6,000-mile oil and filter changes.

new roofline, giving them a more sloping profile. The two-door Fastbacks still had the same look as the 1963½ models.

The 1964 models came with a slightly softer suspension for a smoother ride. According to *Motor Trend* magazine, it also bottomed out "when we crossed rain gutters fairly fast." The writers liked the handling of the four-door 390 V-8 version and said that pumping the tires up to 35 psi made a major improvement over the factory-recommended pressures. "Handling proved above average for a passenger car but then Ford has always rated high in the handling department," they wrote. The Galaxie XL with a 300 horsepower 390 V-8 topped out at 108 mph and accelerated to 60 mph in 9.3 seconds.

The Galaxie 500XL Fastback was the cream of the sports coupes for 1964. It was designed as a sports luxury coupe for the street, and the same body was used for NASCAR racing. For 1964, 923,232 full-sized Fords were produced. (Photos: Ford Motor Company)

1964 Galaxie 500XL

Total Performance was carried over from 1963 as the Ford Division theme. As in the previous year, the 1964 Fords still offered a 427 cubic inch V-8 with either 410 or 425 horsepower—one of the hottest offerings in the industry.

Galaxie 500XL models came with floor-mounted shifters; automatic or manual.

Round tail lamps had long been a Ford styling tradition, except for the 1960 model. The 1964 models dropped the afterburner look and added a gentle slope to the rear end.

Gauges were starting to give way to "idiot lights" by 1964, even in the

The popular two-door Fastback roofline was carried over to the 1964 models and a sloping roof was introduced for the four-door

Ford completely changed the body styling of the 1964 models, including a new grille configuration that was less

The Ford wagons all came with a power rear tailgate window that could be controlled from the driver's seat or with a key at the tailgate. The nine-passenger Country Squire wagon pricing started at $3,088. (Photo: Ford Motor Company)

While Galaxie 500XL models came standard with the 289 V-8, most were ordered with either the potent 352 or 390 cubic inch engine.

The Galaxie 500 four-door hardtops were second in production only to the 500 Fastback model. These sedans provided families with a good compromise between sportiness and practicality. (Photo: Ford Motor Company)

The magazine also tested a dual four-barrel 425 horsepower 427 Galaxie, stripped of everything but performance options. They pointed out that it was happy using progressive linkage to run on only one four-barrel carburetor, lugging along at 30 mph without any overheating. Their test car turned in a 95 mph quarter mile run in 15.4 seconds. The zero-to-60 mph time was 7.4 seconds with a 4.11 rear axle. The big V-8 managed only between eight and 12 mpg for fuel economy. All Ford V-8 engines came with an automatic choke in 1964. You could buy the single-carburetor version, with 410 horsepower, for an additional $461 or purchase the dual-carb 425 hp version for an extra $570.

The Galaxie 500XL convertible was the envy of any neighborhood. The XL convertibles came equipped with vinyl bucket seats, a console-mounted four-speed or automatic and a new standard glass rear window. (Photo: Ford Motor Company)

The Ford warranty in 1964 covered the vehicle for 24 months or 24,000 miles, whichever came first. This warranty was first applied to the Lincoln Continental on October 31, 1960. (Photo: Ford Motor Company)

Galaxie power plants included the Mileage Maker Six, standard on all but the 500XL models, the 289 V-8, the 352 and 390 V-8s and the powerhouse 427 V-8 with 410 or 425 horsepower.

There were 16 full-size Ford models for 1964, including Galaxie 500 hardtops and sedans, Galaxie convertibles, Ford Custom sedans and Ford station wagons.

1964 Ford Options

300 hp 390 V-8	246.00
Cruise-O-Matic	189.60
Electric clock	14.60
Push-button AM/FM radio	83.70
Swing-away steering wheel	50.00
Speed control system	63.40
Whitewall tires	33.90
Equa-Lock differential	42.50

Falcon

The Falcon for 1964 got a sharp-edged, boxy look, losing the soft curving lines of its first three years of production. Sales also began a long decline with the new model, dropping some 29,000 units. This was possibly due to more offerings in both the Fairlane and Mustang lines, siphoning off potential Falcon customers.

Engines for the Falcon were the same as in 1963, with an 85 horsepower, 144 cubic inch six-cylinder standard on most models. Optional 170 or 200 cubic inch I-6 engines were available. All six-cylinder power plants used a single venturi carburetor and ran on regular fuel. The top-of-the-line engine option was the Challenger 260 V-8 with 164 horsepower. The Challenger came standard in the Sprint models, had an automatic choke and ran on regular fuel. The optional fully synchronized four-speed transmission could be mated to any of Falcon's engines, including the Challenger V-8.

Bucket seats and center console were extra-cost options for Sprint. Falcon convertibles continued to use plastic rear windows and came standard with fully powered top operation.

1964 Falcon Options

Fordomatic	167.40
Push-button radio	58.50
Power steering	86.30
Two-tone paint	19.40
Bucket front seats & console	120.50
Wheel covers	16.00
Wire wheel covers	45.10
Vinyl top (hardtops)	75.80
Padded dash and visors	21.80

Fairlane

Fairlane for 1964 carried styling changes similar to big brother Galaxie. It had a similar grille and rounded front quarter panels, although the rear fenders and tail lamps were more similar to the 1963 Galaxie.

Ford claimed that much of the Fairlane appeal came from its extensive option list, making it suitable for someone looking for a Falcon but with more room, or for a high-performance buyer wanting never to be embarrassed in a street race.

Five different engine combinations were offered, ranging from the lowly 170 cubic inch six-cylinder all the way up to the newly available 289 V-8. The 170 was still pumping out 101 horsepower and came standard with the three-speed manual transmission. The 200 six with 116 horsepower was standard if you ordered Fordomatic. The Challenger 260 V-8 was a $100 option, and you could move up to the 195 horsepower 289 V-8 for $145.

Falcon body styling was moving away from the soft lines of previous models, featuring sharper edges. Engine offerings included three six cylinders and the Challenger 260 V-8. (Photo: Ford Motor Company)

Those truly wanting to make a change in their driving lifestyle had to fork over a big chunk of change—$422 for the 271 horsepower 289 V-8. This particular engine came with high-compression heads, high-lift camshaft, dual exhausts, low-restriction intake manifold, solid valve lifters, chrome plated valve stems and a four-barrel carburetor. Compression on the HiPo 289 was 10.5:1 until April

1964, when it was lowered to 10.0:1 with a larger intake valve, leaving the horsepower rating unchanged. A four-speed manual or new three-speed Cruise-O-Matic transmission was available with the 289 V-8. The 271 hp 289 V-8 was available only with the four-speed until later in the year when the Cruise-O-Matic was added to the option list. The two-speed Fordomatic was available for all non-271 hp models.

Falcon sales had slowed steadily since its introduction. From a high production of 497,166 (including Rancheros) in 1961 it had dropped to 318,086 in 1964. (Photo: Ford Motor Company)

Fairlane was growing up, with exciting new options and power offerings, including a hot Challenger 289 V-8 with 271 horsepower.

The base Fairlane four-door model could be expected to average around 19 mpg with the 195 horsepower 289 V-8, according to Motor Trend *magazine. (Photos this page: Ford Motor Company)*

During one magazine road test, the basic Fairlane sports coupe with a 289 weighed in at more than 3,500 pounds. This was heavy for a mid-size unitized construction model, even in 1964. With the stock suspension, the Fairlane leaned excessively in the corners but still gave the test driver a sense of control. Economy on the 289 V-8 with the two-barrel averaged 19.1 mpg on the highway.

1964 Fairlane Options

271 hp 289 V-8	421.80
Cruise-O-Matic	189.60
4-speed (w/289 V-8 only)	188.00
All tinted glass	40.30
Power steering	86.30
Power brakes	43.20
Vinyl top (hardtops)	75.80
Courtesy light group	25.10
Wire wheel covers	45.10
Two tone paint	22.00
Push button radio	58.50

Thunderbird

Thunderbird received its three-year makeover in 1964, moving further into the sports luxury category. The completely new body style lost its tradition of stretching beyond the rest of the lineup. In years past it had always been Thunderbird that provided a glimpse into Ford's future, with its styling and features showing

Thunderbird was completely restyled for 1964 but lost much of previous T-Birds' flair. The sports luxury coupe was now targeting upper-income, older buyers. (Photo: Ford Motor Company)

Thunderbird for 1964
So different ... so beautifully different!

Even Thunderbird advertising pictured people in formal wear, indicating this was a car you would drive to the opera. Of all Ford's engine offerings, the 1964 T-Bird could be bought only with the 300 horsepower 390 V-8.

According to Ford Design Vice President Gene Bordinat, Ford didn't want Mustang to look like a T-Bird or a sedan. "What we really wanted was a car with the look of Total Performance." (Photo: Ford Motor Company)

up on other models a year or two later. Now, the look had moved soundly toward the conservative side but sales didn't slow in the least. More than 92,000 customers flocked to buy the new Thunderbird, up almost 30,000 over the slowing 1963 sales.

The Hardtop, Landau and Convertible models were still the three basic offerings. Standard equipment included power brakes and steering, swing-away steering wheel and column, MagicAire heater, retractable front seat belts and underbody sound coating.

The T-Bird's interior was re-designed, although the familiar layout with bucket seats and a full-length console was still in place.

The 300 horsepower 390 V-8 coupled with Cruise-O-Matic was the only power train available. The high-compression 390 V-8 ran on premium fuel and came standard with dual exhausts, hydraulic valve lifters and a four-barrel carburetor.

Options for the new Thunder-bird ranged from SelectAire conditioner and tinted glass to leather seat bolsters and chrome wire wheels.

1964 Thunderbird Options

Push-button AM/FM radio	83.70
Two-tone paint	25.80
Reclining passenger seat	38.60
Power windows	106.20
Tonneau cover	269.00
Wire wheels	415.20
Transistorized ignition	51.50
Speed control	63.40

Mustang

Lee Iacocca, the 36-year-old vice president of Ford Division, envisioned the success of Mustang early on. He backed up his ideas with market research and went to Henry II and the board of directors to sell it. In a 1964 *Detroit Free Press* article Iacocca said, "I had this thing in my mind from the day I walked into the office." Iacocca had been named a corporate vice president and head of Ford Division in 1961 as the country entered the youth movement of the baby boomers. The postwar babies were all maturing and would shortly be of an age to start purchasing their own vehicles. Iacocca told the board Mustang would be a $50 million project, which he finally

convinced them could sell an extra 100,000 cars a year.

Designed as a low-priced car with high style and economy of operation, Mustang was a vehicle that could flex to meet the needs of many buyers. It could look sporty even at its base level, stripped of options. And for a few dollars more, it could be a fire breathing, 271 horsepower street racer with dual exhausts and sports suspension.

The young vice president put Ford's Advanced Design Studio to work on the project right away, but Henry II apparently was not impressed with any of their designs. Iacocca was getting

Ford Engines for 1964

CID	Carb	Comp.	HP
144 I-6	1 bbl	8.7	85 @ 4200
170 I-6	1 bbl	8.7	101 @ 4400
200 I-6	1 bbl	8.7	116 @ 4400
223 I-6	1 bbl	8.4	138 @ 4200
260 V-8	2 bbl	8.7	164 @ 4400
289 V-8	2 bbl	8.7	195 @ 4400
289 V-8	4 bbl	9.0	210 @ 4400
289 V-8	4 bbl	10.5	271 @ 6000
352 V-8	2 bbl	9.3	250 @ 4400
390 V-8	4 bbl	10.1	300 @ 4600
427 V-8	4 bbl	11.6	410 @ 5600
427 V-8	2x4 bbl	12.0	425 @ 6000

1964 Mustang Convertible

desperate to keep the project moving along, afraid it might die a slow death without a sensational body design. He told Ford Design Vice President Gene Bordinat that he wanted the sporty car design project turned over to the Lincoln-Mercury, Ford and Advanced Studio and "let's have a free for all on it."

The Ford Design Studio team knew there was frantic work happening on the new "sporty car" project but had not been allowed to work on it to that point. Joe Oros was heading up the Ford Design Studio at the time. He was a well-known talent who had provided a strong hand in every Ford design since 1949 and was itching to have a go at the new car.

"I was in the Ford Studio directing some of the new models and I watched this car—it was the 'sporty car'—that was the terminology for it," said Oros. "It was going on in the Advanced Studio and Mr. Ford was not buying anything on the advanced [Mustang] Ford. I'm assuming he wasn't very much impressed and also he had been recently burned with the Edsel. I watched this

for about eight months just wishing I had a chance at it, but I couldn't because it was in the Advanced Studio."

Oros went to an off-site seminar one day, and when he phoned in to the office for messages they had news for him. "They said, 'You know, you won't believe it, Joe, but we've been requested by Mr. Iacocca to compete for the design of the

sporty car.' I said, 'Oh, brother, that's great!' I'd been chafing at the bit to get a hold of that, so a few days later I arrived in the studio and said, 'What are you doing first?' They said, 'Well, we've found a buck and we hope to have something ready for you when you come back on Monday.'

Ford marketing had determined that the new car should have a long hood, short deck and

Mustang hits the starting line full bore!

Most manufacturers illustrated their print ads with vehicles shown lower and wider than the actual cars. Mustang was no exception, and the new pony car sold like hotcakes.

1964 Model Car Pricing

Falcon

2-door Sedan	$1,985
Futura 4-door Sedan	$2,165
Sprint Hardtop	$2,314
Sprint Convertible	$2,586
Wagon 4-door	$2,349
Squire Wagon	$2,611

Fairlane

4-door Sedan I-6	$2,224
4-door Sedan V-8	$2,324

Fairlane 500

4-door Town Sedan I-6	$2,306
4-door Town Sedan V-8	$2,406
Sports Coupe 2-door Hardtop V-8	$2,591

Custom 500

4-door Sedan I-6	$2,507
4-door Sedan V-8	$2,616

Galaxie 500

4-door Sedan I-6	$2,667
4-door Sedan V-8	$2,776

Galaxie 500XL

4-door Sedan	$3,287
Club Victoria 2-door	$3,222
Convertible	$3,484

Mustang 1964½ and 1965 models

Coupe I-6	$2,368
Convertible I-6	$2,614
Fastback I-6	$2,589

Station Wagons

Country Squire 9-passenger	$3,088

Thunderbird

Coupe	$4,486
Landau	$4,589
Convertible	$4,853

THE MOST EXCITING THING ON TV TONIGHT WILL BE A COMMERCIAL

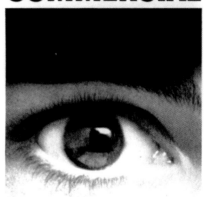

Ford used this print ad in major newspapers across the United States to reveal the new Mustang on prime-time television.

late-1950 Mercury rear window that slanted inward toward the passengers. "I thought, 'My gosh, you guys are crazy. We're supposed to be doing something that is brand-new in appearance.' I never cared for it—it just looked gawky." When Oros viewed the front of the design, he realized it was so chrome heavy that Ford could never afford to produce it.

That particular clay model didn't suit Oros, and he asked one of the designers to cover it with a tarp. "Meet with me and the managers in my office, and we'll talk about this car," said Oros. "I told them why I didn't like it and I said, 'We're not going to win the ball game this way. First of all we can't afford the front end—it's all bumper stock and too darned heavy for the front end of a light car.' I told them that we were in the wrong end of the woods and I just stopped it."

He next brought all the designers in from the Ford studios—designers for trucks, T-Birds and cars and his own advanced section. He wanted them all in the same room to talk about what the car should be. "I had every one of them speak up—there were about 25 of them there." He then took out his notebook with Ford Division's description based on the marketing surveys. "I said I'd like to see something on the front of this car that has the quality of an Italian front end, like a Ferrari grille. I wanted a strong motif in the center of it like the Maserati, but not a copy of it. I'd like the C-pillar to look formal, but not a reverse backlight like the [English Ford] Anglia. For the side elevation I would like to have some indication of a scoop that comes off the design of the jets of World War II to take in air for the rear brakes. That was my formula and we started from scratch and we all went to work."

The designers all worked from seven in the morning to

nine each night for the first week, and in that time they found the correct formula. They had the side elevation right and integrated a scoop intended to cool the rear brakes. Oros said they "hit the front end properly," satisfying his interpretation of Iacocca's new car. "I gave them the cues," said Oros of his team, "and we hit it in the first week." Then he put three teams of clay modelers on three shifts working around the clock to ready the design by the approval date. The team called its design the Cougar and the name stuck right up to the last minute. Oros' Ford Studio team prepared only one car, while each of the other studios had more than one design to show.

sporty qualities. They didn't want a macho look because they wanted both women and men to consider buying the new car. Joe wanted to see what the designers had been working on before starting a new design. There were mere weeks to go before the choice would be made, and he needed to see if there was anything to start working from. "I was the first one to open the design center that morning," said Oros, "and at the studio I noticed they had started a design that did not have any sculptured details on the body side to speak of. The first thing that hit me was that it had a reverse backlight." This was similar to the

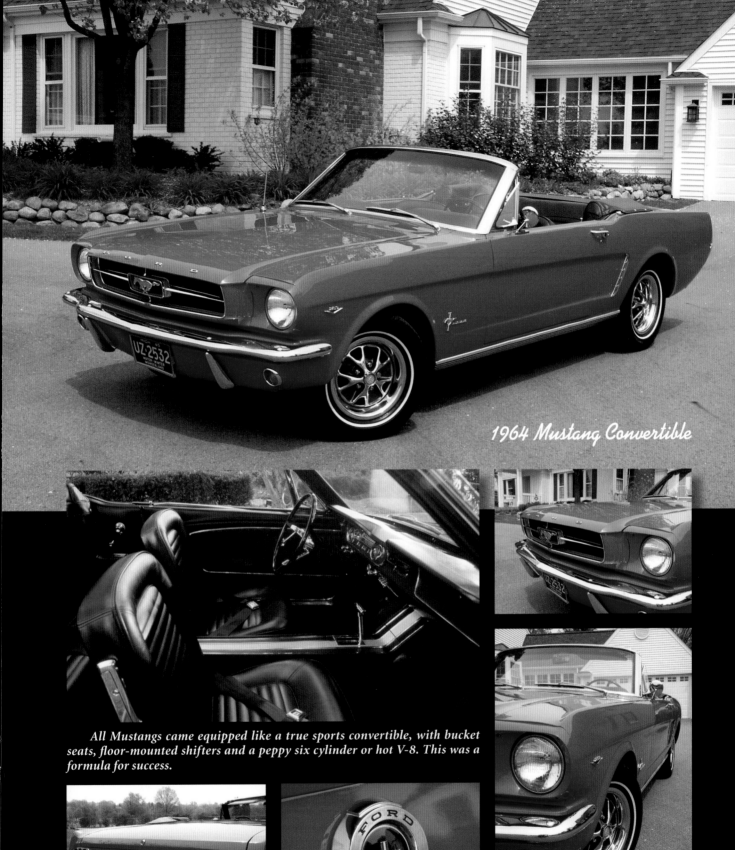

1964 Mustang Convertible

All Mustangs came equipped like a true sports convertible, with bucket seats, floor-mounted shifters and a peppy six cylinder or hot V-8. This was a formula for success.

The simple rear end design gave the Mustang a light, sporty look.

Ford cars favored rear-center gas fillers. This Mustang cap also became a popular theft item early on.

Joe Oros directed his design team to create a car with a long hood and short deck, delivering a "sporty car" look for Lee Iacocca.

1964 Mustang Convertible

Introduced in dealer showrooms on April 17, 1964, the Mustang broke all Ford sales records, selling 1,000 vehicles a day for the first 100 days.

With the car all but finished, Ford Division executives had to pick a name. This front grille sported a Cougar, designer Joe Oros' choice.

With the interior layout finished, only the name badging had to be finalized.

Torino was one of the three final choices for a name, as were Cougar and Mustang. This model had Torino badging on the hubcaps. (Photos this page: Ford Motor Company)

Approval Day

On August 16, 1962, the full-scale clay models from each team were all in the courtyard. The courtyard is an asphalt lot fully encircled by the Ford Design Center so the outside world cannot see what is in Ford's future. It is often used for displaying new models for the top brass. Top management, including Henry II and Iacocca, were there to view the seven entries in the winner-take-all sweepstakes. "We had one car," said Oros, "Advanced Studio had four and Lincoln-Mercury had two. In total there were seven cars out there. I told the guys, 'We don't want another Easter egg.' I wanted the car white because all the other cars Mr. Ford was turning down were painted colors. And all the other cars out in the courtyard were different colors."

"Ours was quite unique and it took the whole ball game. It was a unanimous decision to accept the car we had prepared. They approved everything on our car—no criticisms." Henry II was totally sold on the Oros team design, and Iacocca was just happy he was finally going to have a car.

"I was not in the courtyard at the approval moment, nor was any other chief of a studio there," noted Oros. Henry Ford II walked over later and told Oros, "Joe, you know we've approved your car but you're $15 over the hill on it." Oros said he understood and would find a way to get the money back out of it. The product planners had an established budget and sales band on each car. So the Mustang estimated production cost had to be met or it wouldn't be profitable.

Henry II then wandered over to the seating buck, a mockup of the Mustang interior, and tried out the rear seat. "He was a big man sitting in the rear seat," said Oros. "He said, 'Joe, I believe that we need a little more headroom.' He swung back and hit his head. "I said, 'Yes, sir, we can do that.' And he said, 'Can you do that without losing the design?' and I said, 'Yes, sir, we'll do that,' and that was it. It worked." You didn't want to say no to the guy with his name on the building, according to Oros.

The Ford Division advertising agency of record, J. Walter Thompson, sent a team to the Detroit Public Library and amassed 6,000 possible names for the new vehicle. The early finalists were Colt, Bronco, Puma, Cheetah and Cougar. But the number-one name turned out to be Mustang, with Cougar placing second. Torino was also considered late in the game and even showed up on some of the early mock-ups of the approved design.

"What we did was take the Falcon and give it a tuxedo instead of a normal suit." The goal for Mustang was to bring it in around U.S. $1 per pound. "It was probably one of the most successful cars ever introduced. No one ever thought it would be that successful," said Oros, who now is probably remembered more for the Mustang than for any other car.

Motor Trend published an article titled "Future Total Performance" in February 1964, prior to the Mustang launch. Their investigative work said the car would be called Turino—not Torino—and would be Ford's four-seat answer to Chevrolet's Corvette. The writer said Ford would sell the new car for around $3,000, overestimating the Mustang's entry price by some $700. They did have the Fairlane/Falcon components and power train correct and their sketches were in the ball park.

Ford produced the first Mustang off the Rouge Plant assembly line on March 9, 1964. The company had spent $3.5 million converting the facility for both the Mustang and the Fairlane. Before production started, Ford marketing had determined they could move around 100,000 Mustangs annually. As production startup neared, the estimates were raised to 180,000 and then 240,000.

The San Jose, California, plant was also assigned to Mustang, bringing potential capacity up to 360,000. Shortly after production started, the Metuchen, New Jersey, plant was also converted for more Mustangs, so now capacity was at 440,000.

The Aurora concept show car was first shown publicly at the New York World's Fair dream car exhibit. It featured a television, three AM/FM radios, a tape recorder and built-in beverage cooler. The front passenger seat could swivel to face rear passengers during travel.

The 600 horsepower Ford Gas Turbine Truck was a concept that could run 600 miles at turnpike speeds between refuelings. Actually designed to run on the open roads, the Turbine had the look of the future. (Photos this page: Ford Motor Company)

With sales going through the roof, Ford watched closely to see if Mustang was cannibalizing any of its other car lines. Simply trading sales of one car for another wouldn't be a success. As it happened, though, the entire Ford Motor Company market share jumped from 23.9 percent to 27.1 percent in the first year. It was an amazing increase and Mustang had provided almost all of the improvement.

Ford Division rolled out the Mustang at the 1964 New York World's Fair, and it was in dealer showrooms on Friday, April 17. Ford had a huge promotional program lined up for the new star car, including advance secretive test drives for key magazine editors, timed for articles to hit the newsstands on introduction day. Ford also bought prime-time television ads on all three major networks for April 16 from 9:30 to 10:00 PM, making contact with more than 28 million American viewers. The Mustang ads played on *Hazel, Perry Mason* and *Jimmy Dean*. Ford newspaper ads that morning said, "The most exciting thing on TV tonight will be a commercial," listing the shows and times. And Iacocca and the Mustang appeared on nearly identical covers of *Newsweek* and *Time* on the same day. Ford also moved early on to nail down Mustang as the official pace car for the 1964 Indianapolis 500 on May 30, driven by Benson Ford.

1964 Car Production

Fairlane

4-door Sedan Standard	36,693
2-door Sedan Standard	20,421

Fairlane 500

4-door Sedan	86,919
2-door Sedan	23,447
2-door Hardtop	42,733
2-door Hardtop, Bucket Seats	21,431

Fairlane 500 Wagons

Wagon, Standard	20,980
Custom Wagon	24,962

Falcon

4-door Sedan Standard	27,722
2-door Sedan Standard	36,441
4-door Sedan Deluxe	26,532
2-door Sedan Deluxe	28,411
4-door Sedan Futura	38,032
2-door Sedan Futura	16,621
2-door Sedan Futura, Bucket Seats	212
Futura Hardtop	32,608
Futura Hardtop, Bucket Seats	8,322
Futura Hardtop, Bucket Seats, no console	285
2-door Sprint, Bucket Seats	10,001
2-door Sprint, Bench Seats	3,829

Falcon convertibles

Convertible	13,220
Convertible, Bucket Seats	2,980
Convertible Sprint, Bucket Seats	3,652
Convertible Sprint, Bench Seats	626

Falcon Sedan Delivery

Standard	776
Deluxe	98

Falcon Ranchero

Standard	9,916

Deluxe	7,165
Deluxe, Bucket Seats	235

Falcon Wagons

4-door Wagon Standard	17,779
2-door Wagon Standard	6,034
4-door Wagon Deluxe	20,697
4-door Squire	6,766

Ford Custom

2-door Sedan	41,359
4-door Sedan	57,964

Ford Custom 500

4-door Sedan	68,828
2-door Sedan	20,619

Ford Wagons (4-doors)

Country Sedan 6-passenger	68,578
Country Sedan 9-passenger	25,661
Country Squire 6-passenger	23,570
Country Squire 9-passenger	23,120

Galaxie 500

4-door Sedan	198,805
2-door Sedan	13,041
4-door Hardtop Fastback	49,242
2-door Hardtop Fastback	206,998
Convertible	37,311

Galaxie 500XL

4-door Hardtop Fastback	14,661
2-door Hardtop Fastback	58,306
Convertible	15,169

Mustang

2-door Hardtop	92,705
Convertible	28,833

Thunderbird

2-door Hardtop	60,552
2-door Landau	22,715
Convertible	9,198

| **Total** | **1,733,781** |

Mustang was officially marketed as a 1965 vehicle so Ford could claim huge sales for the first model year—a 17-month period. Sales were more than Ford or Iacocca could have ever hoped for—100,000 Mustangs sold in the first 100 days. Having more than a full month's production in place, Ford had a lot of the new cars to ship but quickly found that they could not keep up with customer demand. Fortunately, they had moved to open up both the California and New Jersey plants for production and soon saw that they would need all of the Dearborn assembly capacity as well. Fifty-three percent of the cars traded in for Mustangs were non-Ford products—a sure sign of success. "I can say," said Iacocca, "that in my 18 years with Ford I've never seen such enthusiasm for a new product."

Concepts

Ford opened the Wonder Rotunda at the New York World's Fair on April 22, 1964, and used it as a tool to introduce new products and future products to the young and old. The Walt Disney–designed facility gave Ford a chance to instill positive feelings and excitement about the company in millions of Americans.

One of the new concept vehicles on display was the Aurora, a new vision in station wagons. It was a futuristic wagon outfitted with television, radio and refrigerator to create a more comfortable environment during long trips, according to Ford Design Vice President Gene Bordinat. It also came with three separate AM/FM radios, a tape recorder, a polarizing sunroof and a built-in beverage cooler cabinet. The central lounge featured a swivel seat, a curved sofa and a children's "romper room." Today's seat belt proponents might have looked disapprovingly on children romping around in a moving vehicle. Those noisy children could also be isolated with a power glass partition.

Other cars shown at the Ford display included the Allegro I, Cougar II and various Mustang concepts supporting the introduction of the actual Mustang at the fair.

▶

While Thunderbird sales continued strong, Mustang was still the big story in 1965. As Thunderbird got heavier and slower, Mustang just got faster.

FORD

The 1965 model year brought continued success to the recently introduced Mustang. Three models were available starting at $2,368 for the six-cylinder coupe.

The Year 1965

Henry Ford II and Lee Iacocca kept Ford Motor Company on track for a fourth consecutive record year in 1965. Worldwide sales hit U.S. $11.5 billion as Ford pushed its sales up by 13 percent. The auto industry as a whole increased only 10 percent.

In North America, more new Ford cars and trucks were sold than ever before. Combined Ford U.S. and Canadian car sales were up an amazing 19 percent from the previous 1964 record. Ford was also halfway through a four-year expansion program to modernize its worldwide facilities. This $2.7 billion program included a new 2.5 million square foot stamping plant in Woodhaven, Michigan.

Having purchased the Philco Corporation in 1961, Henry II proudly pointed out to stockholders that the Philco-built NASA Mission Control Center coordinated the successful Gemini space rendezvous in 1965 and also developed an electronic United States ZIP code reader for the Postal Service. Ford also entered a new phase of recycling in 1965, arranging to purchase scrap steel from junkyard cars to reuse in production, slowing the problem of unsightly auto graveyards.

Ford Motor Company's total employment was up for the year and the average Ford U.S. employee pay rate was now $3.56 per hour.

Lee Iacocca and Don Frey both got promotions early in 1965, moving Iacocca up to chief of the Car and Truck Group and bringing his second in command, Frey, into the Ford Division General Manager position.

New features for 1965 included the vertical headlamps in the Galaxie models, softer lines on the Fairlane and not much of change in the Falcon or Thunderbird. Mustang was still the hot news, and with a new Fastback model and GT option package, it was just what the public wanted.

Galaxie/Custom

Ford introduced the new LTD series for 1965, going to vertical headlamp styling for the first time and hexagonal-shaped tail lamps instead of the traditional round lamps. Ford also introduced reversible ignition keys capable of being inserted either side up.

The frame and suspension were also new in the full-size lineup this year. Coil springs were at all four corners now for a fully independent suspension. Tubular shocks were mounted inside the front coil springs, and the rear suspension used three longitudinal arms to control the fore-and-aft axle position.

The new Galaxie 500 LTD series was now the top-of-the-line big Ford, coming in either a two- or four-door hardtop. The LTD models came standard with a 200 horsepower 289 V-8 and Cruise-O-Matic transmission. The interior was plush "biscuit and pleated" design with large retention buttons. These were the type of seats you could really sink down into. The rear seat came with a fold-down armrest, and there were various touches of simulated walnut, chrome strips and LTD insignias located at various places in the interior.

For the less affluent buyer, Ford offered the Custom and Custom 500 sedans. These models provided the same new frame and suspension components as the Galaxie models but with less plush seating and simulated walnut on

In yet another completely new body design, the full-sized Ford sedans broke new ground with vertical headlamps. The 240 cubic inch I-6 with 150 horsepower was standard on all but the 500XL and LTD models.

the dash. You could still purchase any of the optional power plants including the 425 horsepower 427 V-8 if you wanted a real hot rod.

The interior dash panel was now five inches farther away from the driver than in 1964. Ford said it created a feeling of "spaciousness" in the front seat area. All numbers and letters on the instruments were white on a black background. When the optional SelectAire conditioner was ordered, a different dash came with the car. It added four air vents that incorporated the air conditioning, heater and fresh air.

Ford incorporated a silent flow ventilation system into their four-door hardtop models. The rear vents were located just behind the rear window in front of the deck lid in a negative-pressure area to draw stale air from the interior of the car.

Ford Country Sedan and Country Squire Wagons for 1965 came with two inward-facing, opposing rear seats. The seats folded down flat for storage when not in use.

Power for the new Ford started with a 150 horsepower 240 "Big Six" as standard equipment for all but the Galaxie 500XL and LTD models. Those came with the 200 horsepower 289 V-8. Optional engines for all models except the wagons were the 250 horsepower 352 V-8, the 300 horsepower 390 V-8 and the 425 horsepower 427 V-8. The 427 V-8 was not available in the wagons.

1965 Ford Options

425 hp 427 V-8	570.60
300 hp 390 V-8	246.60
Cruise-O-Matic	189.60
4-speed manual transmission	188.00
Overdrive	108.40
Power steering	97.00
Power brakes	43.20
Power windows	102.10
Electric clock	14.60
Limited slip differential	42.50
Full tinted windows	40.30
SelectAire conditioner	363.80

Both the Country Sedan and Country Squire wagons seated up to 10 passengers with optional facing rear seats. (Photo: Ford Motor Company)

Falcon Sprint V-8 convertible prices started at $2,660 while the base four-door sedan was listed at $2,038.

The Falcon Sprint Fastback was available with three six-cylinder power plants ranging from 105 to 150 horsepower. The top-option Challenger 289 V-8 produced 200 horsepower, and Cruise-O-Matic or three- or four-speed manual transmissions were available.

The Fairlane 500 Sports Coupe had more trunk space than previous models, and styling changes included smooth, rounded front and rear end treatments. (Photos this page: Ford Motor Company)

Falcon

Falcon saw only minor changes for the 1965 model, as demand continued to fall. Sales for 1965 were almost 80,000 units below the 1964 figures and had been dropping since the introduction of the Mustang. Apparently some Falcon buyers decided to move up to the new pony car, leaving the ranks of Falcon. The company still needed Falcon to fill the compact car position, and because sales were still respectable, it would have to do for a few more years.

The body had no changes from 1964 other than trim. The side molding was simpler than in the previous year, and the car now came with different wheel covers. The Futura received an upgraded interior with vinyl leatherette seating surfaces and a bench seat. Bucket seats were optional. This would be the last year for the Sprint models. Ford manufactured a total of 2,806 Sprint hardtops and 300 Sprint convertibles, making each a collector's item.

The 170 cubic inch six producing 105 horsepower was the standard engine, and the seven-main bearing 200 I-6 with 120 horsepower was optional. This year Falcon could also be ordered with the 200 hp 289 V-8 with a two-barrel carburetor. Cruise-O-Matic was optional with any of the Falcon engines and the four-speed transmission was available only with the 289 V-8. The two-speed Fordomatic was finally dropped for 1965.

Falcon's Ranchero had continued to sell consistently since its introduction in 1960. Moving more than 19,000 of the light-duty car/trucks, Ford was filling a need for small businesses and families that needed a double-duty vehicle for transportation and home improvement. It was also respectable enough to drive to the store or to church on a Sunday morning. With an optional 200 horsepower 289 V-8, the Ranchero could reach 60 mph in 10.6 seconds and average about 20 mpg at 65 mph on the freeway. Top speed with the 200 hp V-8 was 99 mph. A limited slip differential was also available with any model and engine combination.

Driving a Falcon was considered a value choice. It was not exciting but provided good, solid transportation for the price. If you wanted value in a sporty car, Mustang was now the choice.

For 1965, Thunderbird again came in three different two-door models: Hardtop, Convertible and Landau. The heavy-duty Cruise-O-Matic transmission was standard.

1965 Falcon Options

200 hp 289 V-8	108.00
Cruise-O-Matic	172.30
Push-button radio	58.50
Power steering	86.30
Ford air conditioner	257.50
Full tinted windows	27.00
Retractable front seat belts	7.55
Wire wheel covers	45.10
Vinyl top (hardtops)	75.80

Fairlane

Styling for the new Fairlane models was softer at all corners than the previous year's styling. Ford continued with the horizontal headlamps, moved to rectangular tail lamps and came up with a design that had less character than the 1964 edition. Minor changes for Fairlane included low-profile tires, reworked steering and more power. Ford also added more sound deadening to isolate the passenger compartment from road noise.

Power for Fairlane came in four flavors for 1965. Standard was the 120 horsepower 200 I-6, and the 289 V-8 engine was an extra-cost option. The 289 V-8 came in three different configurations: The 200 hp two-barrel version offered with a three-speed manual or Cruise-O-Matic, 225 hp high-compression (10.0:1) with a four-barrel using premium fuel, and the 271 hp version, often referred to as the "HiPo," mated with either a four-speed manual or Cruise-O-Matic.

1965 Fairlane Options

271 hp 289 Challenger V-8	429.80
Cruise-O-Matic	179.80
4-speed manual transmission	188.00
Overdrive	108.40
Full tinted windows	31.40
Power steering	86.30
Power brakes	43.20
SelectAire conditioner	363.80

Thunderbird

Ford didn't make many changes to the Thunderbird for 1965. Sales had dropped from more than 92,000 units in 1964 to nearly 75,000 units, showing a serious decline in interest for the sports luxury model. The new model mostly had chrome detail pieces moved around with no body panel changes.

The Thunderbird convertible came with a dome light, power vent windows, retractable seat belts, front disc brakes, sequential turn signals and a reversible key that could be inserted with either side up.

1965 Thunderbird Convertible

1965 Thunderbird Convertible

The Roadster package was still offered for those looking for something unique to set their T-Bird apart from the rest.

The beautifully finished Thunderbird interior included thin shell bucket seats. The passenger seat back reclined completely, allowing the occupant to snooze while listening to the optional five-button AM/FM radio.

Now in its second year of a new body design, Thunderbird came with the

The hydraulic system used for the trunk-stored convertible top was similar to the units in the 1957–59

The chrome Thunderbird name and logo were moved from the tail lenses to the body, a chrome inset was added just behind the front wheel opening, wheel covers were new and a Thunderbird logo replaced the full text across the hood for a neater appearance.

The top-of-the-line Landau model had a vinyl roof and simulated wood trim for the interior. All Thunderbirds now

The Thunderbird Landau model was still identified by the vinyl roof and chrome "S" on the pillars. The Landau's base price was $4,589.

Lee Iacocca had just been promoted to vice president over all Ford Motor Company car and truck divisions as a reward for his sales successes, including the new Mustang. Donald Frey, left, was advanced to Iacocca's old position as head of Ford Division. (Photos this page: Ford Motor Company)

1965 Model Car Pricing

Falcon

4-door Sedan	$2,038
4-door Wagon	$2,317
Futura 4-door Sedan	$2,146
Futura Wagon	$2,453
Futura Convertible	$2,428
Sprint Hardtop V-8	$2,425
Sprint Convertible V-8	$2,660
Squire Wagon	$2,608

Fairlane

4-door Sedan I-6	$2,223
4-door Sedan V-8	$2,329

Fairlane 500

4-door Sedan I-6	$2,303
4-door Sedan V-8	$2,409
Sports Coupe V-8	$2,590

Custom

4-door Sedan I-6	$2,366
4-door Sedan V-8	$2,472

Custom 500

4-door Sedan I-6	$2,467
4-door Sedan V-8	$2,573

Galaxie 500

4-door Sedan I-6	$2,623
4-door Sedan V-8	$2,730

Galaxie 500 LTD

4-door Hardtop	$3,313
2-door Hardtop	$3,233

Galaxie 500XL

2-door Hardtop	$3,167
Convertible	$3,426

Mustang 1964½ and 1965 models

Coupe I-6	$2,368
Convertible I-6	$2,614
Fastback I-6	$2,589

Station Wagon

Country Squire 10-passenger	$3,216

Thunderbird

Coupe	$4,486
Landau	$4,589
Convertible	$4,953

came standard with power-assisted front disc brakes, and the only engine offered was the standard 300 horsepower 390 V-8. Cruise-O-Matic was still standard for seamless shifting.

Sequential turn signals were a novelty for Thunderbird, with three bulbs behind each lens operating sequentially from the center to the outside for left or right turns. Thunderbird convertibles now had a dome light in the top rear of the folding soft top for low-light convenience.

1965 Thunderbird Options

SelectAire conditioner	424.90
Power driver's seat	92.10
Power windows	106.20
Limited slip differential	47.70
Full tinted windows	43.00
Automatic speed control	63.40
Reclining passenger seat	45.10
Two-tone paint	25.80
Highway pilot control	128.72
Vacuum truck lid release	12.90

Mustang

When Mustang was introduced, it hit first place in compact sales and fourth place overall by the second month. You would think that after six months some of the initial enthusiasm might have dwindled. But Ford dealers loved this new model, finding that hordes of customers from all age groups were still coming into their showrooms. Mustangs brought them in, even if they left with something other than the pony car.

The direct-current generator in the early 1964½ models was replaced by the summer of 1964 with an alternator. By September 1964 there were new additions for the 1965 model lineup, including a new Fastback model, a GT package and Carroll Shelby's GT350. Corvette owners were already wary of the Cobra roadsters, and now they had to watch over their shoulders for Shelby Mustangs.

The 289 V-8, coming in three configurations—200 hp two-barrel, 225 hp four-barrel and 271 hp four-barrel high-performance versions—was now available along with the 260 V-8. The 260 was soon dropped with the 200 horse 289 V-8 taking its place. Standard power for Mustang was now the 200 cubic inch six with 120 horsepower. The passenger seat was adjustable starting with the 1965 model run.

On September 9, 1964, a Ford press release announced the new Fastback model. "The new Mustang 2+2 joins the 1965 Mustang hardtop and convertible model in Ford dealer showrooms Friday, September 25." The 2+2 Mustang was a four-seater, and you could fold down the rear seat backs for extra cargo or luggage capacity. The Fastback had functional air louvers built into the rear roof quarter panels for the flow-through ventilation system. Ford General Manager Don Frey said this "permitted window-up driving free from wind noises and drafts in nearly all kinds of weather."

Magazine writers liked the new concept, saying, "The new Fastback top is smooth, tight and gives a completely different character to the car." With a standard 200 cubic inch I-6 and

manual transmission, the 2+2 weighed in at 2,605 pounds, compared to the convertible at 2,755 pounds. The hardtop was lightest at 2,445 pounds.

A year after Mustang's introduction, a GT equipment package was offered with grille-mounted foglights, front disc brakes, special trim and striping along the lower side panels. The column-mounted Rally Pac tachometer and handling package were also included. If you wanted to further individualize your Mustang you had to order other options including the high-performance V-8 and instrument group.

Motor Trend magazine tested an early high-performance model shipped to California by Ford, loaded with all the new performance options. The hardtop model included the 271 hp 289 V-8, four-speed transmission, handling package, quick steering, 3.89 rear axle and Firestone Super Sport 170-TW racing tires. Running the car at Riverside Raceway, the writers found the 2,980-pound car impressive. Zero-to-60 mph was clocked at 7.5 seconds, the quarter mile was 15.7 seconds at 89 mph and top speed was 117 mph. "Our Mustang had a suspension system that was very firm and comfortable, which

means Ford has come up with quite a package for those willing to wait for it," said writer Bob McVay. "Even with production increased to 28,800 units a month, the waiting periods are still eight weeks in some areas." On the high-performance model, mileage wasn't the Mustang's strong point, ranging from 11.7 in town to 14.6 on the open roads.

All Mustangs still offered bucket seats, nylon carpeting, vinyl seating surfaces, padded dash, full wheel covers and floor-mounted shifters for both manual and automatic transmissions as standard equipment. A full-length console was also available with a lighted front storage compartment and an ashtray and courtesy light at the rear. The air-conditioned models used a unique console without a storage compartment.

1965 Mustang Options

271 hp 289 V-8	442.60
Cruise-O-Matic	189.60
4-speed manual transmission	188.00
Front disc brakes	58.00
Power convertible top	54.10
Full-length center console	51.50
Vinyl roof	75.80
Styled wheels	122.30
Special handling package	31.30
Rally Pac	70.80
Power steering	86.30
Power brakes	43.20

The all-new Mustang 2+2 Fastback had functional louvered air outlets at the rear quarter panels, drafting air through the car even with the windows rolled up.

1965 Mustang Coupe

At $2,368 the new Mustang coupe was a tremendous value. Conceived by Ford Division head Lee Iacocca and his marketing team, the Mustang offered standard bucket seats, a floor-mounted shifter, vinyl seating surfaces and full wheel covers.

Even base-model Mustangs were sporty and well equipped. Ford marketing had the "typical" Mustang buyer pegged as a 31-year-old college-educated professional earning around $8,500 per year.

The rear foam seats would fold down to form a 35 x 41-inch platform.

The standard radio was a manual AM model. For an additional $59 you could have a push-button version.

The standard engine for Mustang was a 200 cubic inch six producing 120 horsepower with a one-barrel carburetor.

The front seating area provided plenty of leg space and comfortable seating.

Vertical bars on the brake lights were subtle and stylish.

The new Fastback added a third model to the Mustang lineup. Ford welded the body to the frame to lessen body squeaks and rattles, and front fenders were bolted on for easy replacement.

The passenger side mirror was optional and dealer installed.

The backseat was meant for small children or very short trips. The seat back folded down to provide a flat cargo area through to the trunk

GA·4040

1965 Mustang Fastback

Shelby Mustangs

By building high-performance cars, Carroll Shelby was doing what he wanted to do while providing a service to Ford Motor Company. After being forced from a successful race driving career in 1961 by a heart ailment, Shelby tried his hand at a driving school but found more success in building Cobra roadsters in California. When the Mustangs came along in April 1964, Ford asked Shelby to consider building a modified version of the new four-seater to go after the SCCA B-Production national championship. They approached him in August 1964 and by September the first GT350 models were built. Although the car would never reach production volumes that Ford would consider profitable, that wasn't the purpose of Shelby's rockets. The GT350, like the Cobra, was meant to win races and give Ford bragging rights in their advertising and marketing through trouncing Corvette and Ferrari.

To meet SCCA rules, Shelby would have to build at least 100 editions of the Mustang to qualify for the production class. Because he needed only a few race cars to get the job done, Shelby laid plans to build two-seat street versions for the general public to buy. This move turned out to be quite profitable for Shelby and reserved a place for him in automotive history.

The starting point was a white Mustang 2+2 equipped from the factory with a 271 hp 289 V-8 and a four-speed. Then Shelby American changed the cam; added a Holley 715 CFM carburetor, high-rise aluminum manifold, cast aluminum oil pan and high-performance headers; and ended up with a 306 hp version of Ford's engine. The GT350 included a Galaxie rear axle, Koni adjustable shocks, faster steering, Goodyear Blue Dot tires, bigger 9.5-inch disc brakes in the front and metallic linings on the 10-inch rear drums. The battery was relocated to the trunk and a fiberglass hood replaced the factory steel for better weight distribution.

Performance from the street racer was excellent. *Motor Trend* writer John Ethridge described firing up the engine for the first time. "You're first impressed with a raucous note from the twin exhausts." He said they were actually louder inside the car because it lacked insulation or undercoating. "Not everyone will appreciate the cockpit noise and firm ride, but we're sure no enthusiast will ever complain." The GT350 averaged 11.2 mpg under hard driving and 17 mpg on the open road. *Motor Trend* clocked a zero-to-60 mph figure of 7 seconds and a top speed of 125 mph at 6,100 rpm.

Inside the GT350 the rear seats were removed, three-inch-wide competition seat belts installed and a mahogany wood-rimmed steering wheel replaced the stock plastic model. The rear seat removal was prompted by SCCA rules that B-Production sports cars be two-seaters. The sticker price on the street package ran $4,547 before tax and delivery.

Shelby's GT350R models were built for competition only, and everything nonessential was pulled out, including carpeting, door panels and the headliner. The glass was replaced with Plexiglas, helping cut more than 200 pounds out of the stock Mustang 2+2. The Shelby American engines produced well over 350 hp, fed by a 34-gallon fuel tank. Not that many enthusiasts had the extra pocket change to buy something not certified for street use at $5,950. Only 32 GT350R models were ever built.

Cobra

The unveiling of the first 427 Cobra was held at Riverside Raceway in January 1965. Development had been under way for some time to produce a big-block Cobra after an initial experiment in June 1964 at Sebring. Shelby's crew had stuffed a 427 in a leaf-spring chassis, and it proved to be quite a handful for driver Ken Miles at Sebring. The car got out of control exiting a turn and hit the only tree on the course. Keeping in mind that the 289, known as the Mark II chassis, had a transverse rear leaf spring and a chassis originally built for an inline six-cylinder, this probably wasn't a marriage made in heaven. But seeing the possibilities prompted Shelby American to start working on an all-new Cobra with a tubular chassis. By late 1964 the new car was under serious development testing in the United Kingdom and later in the States.

Carroll Shelby wanted a chassis that could handle the torque and was built for the Ford 427 wedge engine. "The 427 Cobra had a whole new chassis designed on a computer," said Shelby. "Klaus Arning [Ford engineer] always wanted to build a chassis on a computer, so he worked after hours to put it together. It had anti-squat and anti-dive built in to it." Everything from the 289 Cobra chassis was scrapped except the standard Salisbury rear end. It proved to work perfectly. Using four-inch steel tubing, the 1965 competition body slipped easily on the new chassis without modification.

Ford Engines for 1965			
CID	Carb.	Comp.	HP
170 I-6	1 bbl	9.1	105 @ 4400
200 I-6	1 bbl	9.2	120 @ 4400
240 I-6	1 bbl	9.2	150 @ 4000
260 V-8	2 bbl	8.7	164 @ 4400
289 V-8	2 bbl	9.3	200 @ 4400
289 V-8	4 bbl	10.0	225 @ 4800
289 V-8	4 bbl	10.5	271 @ 6000
352 V-8	2 bbl	9.3	250 @ 4400
390 V-8	4 bbl	10.1	300 @ 4600
390 V-8	4 bbl	10.1	330 @ 5000
427 V-8	2x4 bbl	11.1	425 @ 6000

The 1965 Allegro II concept car was supposed to reflect the coming styles of the Ford Mustang and Mercury Cougar.

The street Cobra 427s sold for $7,495, or you could purchase the race-ready version with a wet sump engine for $9,750. The street version had a curb weight of 2,450 pounds. In a 1965 *Sports Car Graphic* road test, race driver/writer Jerry Titus said he ran the quarter mile speed tests at Riverside Raceway on a strip recently used for a drag event. Apparently a number of cars had dumped oil on the track, hampering his acceleration runs.

"The best we could get with the street machine was 110 mph in 13.2 seconds through the quarter," said Titus. "It was the first street machine we'd ever driven that would keep the tires lit up for the full quarter in every gear. The race car, with its blueprinted engine and huge rear tires, got a full second off of that, blasting through the trap at 6,500 [rpm] in third gear."

Ford was having trouble getting their Ford GT racing program in gear and asked Shelby to take it over. Taking this on while still building GT350 Mustangs and 427 Cobras was just too much. "I had 15 of them [427 Cobras] left when we decided to concentrate on the GT40s," said Shelby. "Nobody wanted them

Allegro II's total height was only 41 inches.

The Cougar II featured a tubular racing frame, Borrani wire wheels, a Challenger 260 V-8 and pop-up headlights. (Photos this page: Ford Motor Company)

so we sold them to a dealer for $5,000 a piece." These all went to Pletcher Ford in Jenkintown, PA. "He called and told me that he had sold five of those for $7,500 each and appreciated making that much money. And a few years later they were selling for more than $800,000 and I'm still a little sick about that!"

There were 126 Cobras built with the worm and sector steering units—75 with the Challenger 260 V-8 and 51 with the 289 V-8. Shelby built 402 Cobras with the 289 V-8 and rack-and-pinion steering. Occasionally a Cobra would be held up on the assembly line waiting for some specialty part ordered by the customer.

1965 Car Production

Fairlane
4-door Sedan Standard	25,378
2-door Sedan Standard	13,685

Fairlane 500
4-door Sedan	77,836
2-door Sedan	16,092
2-door Hardtop	41,405
2-door Hardtop, Bucket Seats	15,141

Fairlane Wagons
500 Model	20,506
Standard	13,911

Falcon
4-door Sedan Standard	30,186
2-door Sedan Standard	35,858
4-door Sedan Deluxe	13,850
2-door Sedan Deluxe	13,824

Falcon Futura
4-door Sedan	33,985
2-door Sedan	11,670
2-door Hardtop	24,451
2-door Hardtop, Bucket Seats	1,303
Convertible	6,191
Convertible, Bucket Seats	124

Falcon Sedan Delivery
Standard	649
Deluxe	112

Falcon Ranchero
2-door Standard	10,539
2-door Deluxe	7,734
2-door Standard, Bench Seats	16
2-door Deluxe, Bench Seats	990

Falcon Sprint
2-door Hardtop, Bucket Seats	2,806
2-door Convertible, Bucket Seats	300

Falcon Wagons
4-door Wagon Standard	14,911
2-door Wagon Standard	4,891
4-door Wagon Deluxe	12,548
4-door Squire Wagon	6,703

Ford Custom
4-door Sedan	96,393
2-door Sedan	49,034

Ford Custom 500
4-door Sedan	71,727
2-door Sedan	19,603

Ford Wagons
Country Squire 9-passenger	30,502
Country Sedan 6-passenger	59,693
Country Sedan 9-passenger	32,344
Ranch Wagon 6-passenger	30,817
Country Squire 6-passenger	24,308

Galaxie 500
4-door Sedan	181,183
4-door Hardtop Fastback	49,982
2-door Hardtop Fastback	157,284
2-door Convertible	31,930

Galaxie 500 LTD
4-door Hardtop Fastback	68,038
2-door Hardtop Fastback	37,691

Galaxie 500XL
2-door Hardtop Fastback	28,141
2-door Convertible	9,849

Mustang
2-door Hardtop, Standard	372,123
2-door Hardtop, Bench Seats	14,905
2-door Fastback, Standard	71,303
2-door Hardtop, Luxury	22,232
2-door Fastback, Luxury	5,776
Convertible, Standard	65,663
Convertible, Bench Seats	2,111
Convertible, Luxury	5,338

Thunderbird
2-door Hardtop	42,652
2-door Landau	25,474
Convertible	6,846
Total	**2,070,537**

This would let cars with later serial numbers roll by and actually come off the line ahead of the stalled Cobra. So if production changed from a 260 V-8 to a 289 V-8 during that time, for example, the lower serial number car could end up with a later engine version. This is why there isn't always logic in figuring out when a car came off the line or what it was equipped with.

Total Cobra 427 production ran from January 1965 to March 1967, with Shelby building about 311 of the classic powerhouse roadsters—260 street versions and 51 competition models. After selling only 21 of the competition models Shelby turned the other 30 into street-legal "Cobra SC" models, selling them to dealers.

Concept Cars

The Allegro II was billed as an open car version of the Allegro I concept coupe. In reality, it was a unique body with a front end that strongly resembled the yet-to-be-produced Chevrolet Camaro and stood only 33 inches from ground to cowl. The rear end was something in advance of a Lotus Europa with a built-in roll bar, flat deck lid and dual exhausts.

The Cougar II was actually introduced in 1964 and was making the show tour throughout 1965. It had clean body lines, an integrated roll bar and a high-performance V-8. (Photo: Ford Motor Company)

▶

By 1966 sales of Mustang had surpassed Ford's wildest dreams. Even though the body style showed little change, the pony car now had a model for everyone, ranging from the standard six to a hot 289 cubic inch V-8.

FORD

The Year 1966

Ford applied subtle changes to the 1966 Mustangs. Mustang featured a new horizontal bar grille, "wind splits" added to the side air scoops, a new gas filler cap and new wheel covers.

Federal regulations for safety and auto emissions standards took effect under the National Traffic and Motor Vehicle Safety Act of 1966. They put pressure on manufacturers to start finding ways to lessen emissions, improve economy and further protect vehicle occupants from that time on. Henry Ford II summed up the act for the Ford shareholders: "The Company's initial experience under the Act makes it clear that henceforth the design of our products and many other aspects of our business will be profoundly influenced by Federal safety regulations."

Ford feared the coming regulations, knowing that the government would be more and more involved in the business of auto manufacturers. All the car makers knew that regulation was coming and started to figure out ways to increase automobile safety and to clean up engine emissions, even though the costs would have to be passed on to the buyer. This challenge severely curtailed performance during the decade of the 1970s.

For 1966 Ford North American sales were still very healthy, second only to its 1965 sales, while worldwide sales had fallen slightly. Ford profits were down, an industry-wide trend, with wages, materials and new safety products being targets

for blame. Ford's American and Canadian car and truck sales totaled 3,239,309 for 1966, down 64,000 units from the previous year.

For 1966 Ford introduced its new Galaxie 7-Litre series and its first SUV, the Bronco. No one had the slightest idea where the little SUV would take Ford on the sales charts years later.

Ford

Galaxie and Custom full-size Fords had a new body with slightly rounded fenders, keeping the vertical headlamp format. A new LTD hardtop with a roofline reminiscent of the 1963 Fastback was introduced. Also in the lineup was a new Galaxie 500 7-Litre model, coming standard, as the name would indicate, with a 428 cubic inch V-8.

The new Ford wagons offered at no extra cost a dual-action rear

hatch, opening as either a door or a tailgate, making it easy to load cargo or passengers from the back.

Engine offerings included the base 155 hp "Standard 6" or a 200 hp "Basic 8." The livelier engine options were the 250 hp 352 V-8, 265 hp 390 V-8, 315 hp 390 V-8, 345 hp 428 (7-Litre) V-8 or the powerhouse 425 hp 427 V-8. The 427 engine was now a $1,074.01 option and not many were built.

The 428 engine in the Ford's 7-Litre model was meant to give some Ford buyers a chance to own a big block they could live with. It came with quieter hydraulic lifters and produced 345 horsepower. With service intervals further apart, it was primarily for the driver who wanted more comfort and less hassle than was involved in owning a 427 V-8. Performance, however, was not its strong point—especially in comparison to driving a Ford equipped with a 427 V-8. *Motor Trend* tested the new 7-Litre model expecting a fast ride. "Making seven liters run as quietly as Rolls apparently stifles some of its potential. And the extra big engine sucks in gas." During their test the big Ford delivered only 13 mpg on the open road and 11.5 mpg in town driving. Their car managed only 9.6 seconds getting to 60 mph and a best quarter-mile speed of 81 mph.

Transmissions were varied, with the fully synchronized three-speed column shift standard on lower models and optional Cruise-O-Matic on all V-8 engines except for the 427 V-8, which came standard with a four-speed manual. Other options included power steering, six-way power bench seat, power tailgate window and a Stereo-Sonic Tape System.

1966 Ford Options

425 hp 427 V-8	1,074.01
250 hp 352 V-8	164.41
Cruise-O-Matic	214.63
4-speed manual transmission	182.69
SelectAire conditioning	353.52
Power disc brakes	96.51
6-way power seat	94.07
Power steering	94.26
Power windows	99.22
Limited slip differential	41.30
Full tinted windows	39.17
Speed control	61.61
Deluxe seat belts, retractors	14.43
Tinted windshield and windows	39.17

Falcon

The new Falcon was now based on the Fairlane chassis but with a shorter wheelbase in the sedan models. Sales continued to drop and without the Sprint models, the Futura Sports Coupe was the most youthful body style offered—no match for the Mustang. The Falcon convertible line was discontinued as well.

Falcon dropped another 29,000 units below the 1965 production level but still came in at a profitable volume with more than 200,000 cars rolling off the line. While Ford may have seen the end of the road for Falcon, it knew there was still going to be a market for an entry-level small car, and Falcon would have to fill that position for a few more years.

Reversible keys were available for the first time on Falcon, inherited when it moved

1966 Timeline

- *Motor Trend* names Mercury Cougar the 1967 Car of the Year
- Ford is first manufacturer to introduce optional eight-track tapes
- The first episode of "Batman" airs on January 12
- Jack Ruby dies in prison
- March 2: One millionth Mustang is built in less than two years from start of production
- Best Picture Oscar: *A Man for All Seasons* starring Paul Scofield

up to the Fairlane platform. The combination heater/air conditioner unit was now integrated into the dash area replacing the earlier under-dash mounting.

With the exception of the Ranchero engines, power came in three versions for 1966. The base engine was the 105 hp 170 six cylinder, the next step up was the 120 hp six and the

Galaxie came in Custom, Custom 500, Galaxie 500, 500XL, LTD and the all-new Galaxie 500 7-Litre models. As the new name indicated, the last came standard with a 428 cubic inch engine in either a fastback or convertible.

The simulated wood trim and moldings made the Ford Country Squire wagons easily identifiable. Pricing for the 9-passenger version started at $3,292. (Photos this page: Ford Motor Company)

top-of-the-line power came from the 200 hp 289 V-8 with a two-barrel carburetor. The four-barrel 225 hp version became available later in the model year. Zero-to-60 mph for the 120 hp six was 17 seconds, while the 200 hp V-8 cut five seconds off that time.

Ranchero was still based on the Falcon body styling, and carried the Falcon name, but was also based on the Fairlane chassis, leaving room for it to grow beyond the small-block engine at any time. Engines for 1966 were still limited to the standard 200 cubic inch six or the 289 V-8.

1966 Falcon Options

200 hp Challenger 289 V-8	104.84
Cruise-O-Matic	167.19
4-speed manual transmission	182.69
Power brakes	41.98
Power steering	83.86
Power tailgate window	31.39
Full tinted windows	30.51
Push-button AM radio	57.03
Two-tone paint	18.85
Wheel covers	21.19
Vinyl roof	73.65

Falcon models came with padded instrument panels, front and rear safety belts and backup lights standard. A child seat could be purchased for an additional $29.95. Other options were SelectAire at $356.09 and tinted glass for $30.51.

The Falcon Futura Sports Coupe became less stylish, and popularity continued to decline. By 1966 total Falcon production was down to 204,429 including Ranchero—less than half of the 1960 production. (Photos this page: Ford Motor Company)

Fairlane

New styling and vertical headlamps freshened up the Fairlane for 1966. One of the earlier problems with the Fairlane was it could take only a small-block V-8 under the hood. When muscle car mania hit, with General Motors taking the lead, Ford was left hanging with nothing to sell but their Galaxie Lightweight, with a 427 V-8. No hot intermediate models were available from Ford dealers.

Therefore, the 1966 Fairlane was redesigned to accommodate the bigger 390 V-8, and even though it was almost two years behind Pontiac's GTO, it was now ready for the challenge. While the basic Fairlane engines, starting with the 120 hp 200 I-6, were still available, the Fairlane GT and GT/A (automatic) models carried two 390 V-8 options: a 315 hp version and the hot 335 hp rubber-burning setup. The GT/A carried the SelectShift Cruise-O-Matic (C6) transmission, which allowed the driver to hold the car in first or second gear until the engine reached redline. This apparently worked well, with reporters saying the control almost matched that of a manual transmission.

The GT and GT/A were quickly recognized on the street as hot models that could cause serious problems for a Pontiac GTO or an Olds 442. Ford upgraded its 390 V-8 to become one of the most wanted muscle engines on the road. By changing a number of internal pieces, Ford boosted the horsepower to 315 or 335, depending on the model you chose. The 335 hp 390 V-8 incorporated a baffled oil pan, new heads and intake manifold, a high-lift camshaft and valve springs, a larger Holley four-barrel carburetor and a low-restriction air cleaner.

Bucket seats, a console-mounted shifter (manual or automatic) and a sound-deadening package that included 120 pounds of insulation came with the GT. Nylon 7.75 x 14 inch tires were mounted on six-inch rims and a heavy-duty suspension with stiffer springs and a larger anti-roll bar accounted for the improved handling.

Motor Trend magazine tested a 1966 GT/A, finding the drum brakes exceptional, even after hard use, and acceleration times that would make any street racer proud. Zero-to-60 mph took a mere 6.8 seconds and they ran the quarter mile in 15.2 seconds at 92 mph. Top speed was 125 mph at 5,100 rpm. Writer John Ethridge commented, "Driving the GT/A, both on acceleration runs and around Ford's Dearborn ride and handling course, was an absolute blast."

Fairlane offered two new models: the 500XL and the potent GT. The 335 hp GT model pricing started at $2,843.

Ford sold 43,763 Fairlane wagons during the 1966 model year. The top-of-the-line Squire model with woodlike grain was listed at $2,901 with a V-8 engine. (Photos this page: Ford Motor Company)

1966 Fairlane Options

335 hp 390 V-8	206.00
Cruise-O-Matic	214.63
Power brakes	41.98
Power steering	83.86
Power tailgate window	31.39
Power convertible top	52.57
Full tinted glass	30.51
Two-tone paint	21.38
Whitewall tires	33.11
Wagon luggage rack	44.12

Thunderbird

Sales for the 1966 Thunderbird were down by 5,796 units, not unexpected because it was in the final model year of a three-year run. Ford, having put all its money into the upcoming 1967 model, did not want to invest heavily in the current Thunderbird and decided to make only minor changes.

While Ford continued with the basic convertible and hardtop models, Thunderbird now had Town Landau and Town Hardtop models with the "Town" designation indicated on an enlarged rear C-pillar that fully blocked the rear passenger windows. The purpose, according

to Ford, was to give rear seat passengers more privacy. It is likely that the modification was nothing more than an inexpensive method of changing the appearance while boasting two new Thunderbird models.

Thunderbird now had an optional engine for the first time since 1960. The 315 hp 390 V-8 was the standard power, but for $64.30 more you could have the 345 hp 428 V-8, the same engine as in the new Galaxie 500 7-Litre model. Cruise-O-Matic was still the only transmission available.

Interior appointments included standard power brakes and steering while power side windows were a $103.20 option. New for the Town Landau and Hardtop was an overhead console panel that indicated low fuel, door open, seat belts unfastened and also incorporated the emergency flasher switch. A child's bucket seat was a $29.95 dealer-installed option.

1966 Thunderbird Options

345 hp 428 V-8	64.30
SelectAire conditioner	412.90
6-way power seat	96.62
Power windows	103.20
Limited slip differential	46.35
Full tinted windows	41.79
AM/FM Stereo-Sonic Tape	127.56
Reclining passenger seat	147.03
Two-tone paint	25.07

Mustang

With Mustang having been on the road for a year and a half, Ford saw no reason to make major waves by changing the formula. The model lineup for 1966 continued with the convertible, hardtop and 2+2 looking very much the same.

Expanding the optional equipment package was the easiest way for Ford to spice up the four-seater and make it even more profitable. The GT equipment option for 1966, as in the previous year, included disc brakes, foglamps, a new GT fuel filler cap, black painted grille, dual exhaust, GT striping, special handling package and the optional 225 hp 289 V-8 or the extra-cost 271 hp version.

All Mustang instrument panels now came with the five-gauge layout previously reserved for the GT equipment option. The 1965 non-GT models had used basic warning lights. The Rally Pac option with steering column–mounted tachometer and clock was still available at extra cost. Another option, primarily to support Ford's image as a company concerned with safety, was a dealer-installed child seat—somewhat ahead of its time.

One of the more popular options in the Mustang was the eight-track Stereo-Sonic Tape System, providing owners with the luxury of listening to their taste in music. Most of the popular artists were rapidly becoming available on the eight-track format and Mustang buyers, according to Ford marketing managers, were "hip." The tape system was integrated with the AM radio, and with rear speakers provided an excellent sound. Deluxe seat belts and warning chimes were also optional, while basic front and rear seat belts were standard.

On Mustang non-GT models Ford removed the large horizontal chrome bar and honeycomb grille, replacing it with small, horizontal bars and a floating horse emblem. Just ahead of the rear wheels, small chrome "wind splits" were mounted in the simulated air scoops. Ford also provided a new look for the wheel covers and rear-mounted gas cap. Coming without the simulated side scoops, the 2+2 model presented a slightly cleaner profile.

The front grille for GT models required a single horizontal chrome bar to support the fog-lamps and horse emblem. The grille was painted black, making the chrome trim, horse and fog-lamps stand out.

Thunderbird offered an eight-track Stereo-Sonic Tape System installed in the wraparound console. Speakers were mounted throughout the interior.

The T-Bird Landau model featured closed-off rear windows. Ford advertised it as a privacy feature. Landau was priced at $4,552 for 1966. (Photos this page: Ford Motor Company)

The Mustang engine lineup saw the 170 cubic inch six dropped late in the 1965 production model run, leaving only two basic engine choices: the 200 cubic inch six or a 289 V-8. The V-8 offered three different horsepower ratings: 200, 225 or 271 hp, enough to satisfy almost any enthusiast's needs. The 271 hp version was now referred to in Ford sales brochures as the Cobra V-8. Recognizing that more vehicles could be sold if something other than four-on-the-floor was offered for the top performer, Ford now made its Cruise-O-Matic transmission available with the top V-8.

The Mustang was still one of Ford's all-time success stories a year and a half after its introduction. Most new models lose their glow after a few months, but not Mustang. During the 1966 model year another 607,568 units were produced to feed a hungry audience, and Ford was working on the second-generation styling, hoping not to mess too much with success.

Optional for 1966 was an eight-track Stereo-Sonic Tape System and deluxe seat belts with a warning light. A steering column–mounted Rally Pac tachometer and clock was again available as a factory option.

Individual taillight lenses were set wider apart for 1966, separated with thin strips of sheet metal. GT models had finned dual exhaust outlets. (Photos this page: Ford Motor Company)

1966 Mustang Options

271 hp 289 V-8	430.39
Cruise-O-Matic	214.63
4-speed manual transmission	182.69
Power brakes	41.98
Power steering	83.86
Full-length console	50.05
Vinyl roof	73.82
Styled wheels	93.16
Special handling package	30.42
Rally Pac	68.80
Limited slip differential	41.30

Ford Engines for 1966

CID	Carb.	Comp.	HP
170 I-6	1 bbl	9.1	105 @ 4400
200 I-6	1 bbl	9.2	120 @ 4400
240 I-6	1 bbl	9.2	155 @ 4200
289 V-8	2 bbl	9.3	200 @ 4400
289 V-8	4 bbl	10.0	225 @ 4800
289 V-8	4 bbl	10.5	271 @ 6000
352 V-8	2 bbl	9.3	250 @ 4400
390 V-8	2 bbl	9.5	265 @ 4400
390 V-8	4 bbl	10.5	315 @ 4600
390 V-8	4 bbl	10.5	335 @ 4800
428 V-8	4 bbl	10.5	345 @ 4600
427 V-8	2x4 bbl	11.1	425 @ 6000

Shelby Mustang

The 1966 GT350 came with minor changes, reverting to an all-steel hood (formerly fiberglass), a horizontal bar grille, rear quarter windows where louvers were before and a new side scoop to provide more air to the rear brakes. The dual exhaust, formerly exiting each side of the car ahead of the rear wheels, now ran straight out the back using fiberglass packed mufflers. Ford's Cruise-O-Matic, known as SelectShift in the Fairlane GT/A, was now available in the GT350 as well.

Shelby American also built 936 GT350H models for Hertz to rent to customers in North America. The Hertz cars came with either four-speed manual or three-speed automatic transmissions and were painted black with gold racing stripes. The automatic-equipped models were sold to Hertz for $4,995.25 including Power-Lok differential, cast alloy wheels, folding rear seat, Le Mans stripe and AM radio.

A July 29, 1966, *Ford World* headline read, "$13 Rents Hertz GT for a Day." Yes, for mere pocket change you could rent a Shelby "rent-a-racer." There was also a charge of 13 cents per mile for the black-and-gold Mustangs compared to an $11 a day, 11-cents-a-mile charge for other Hertz cars. Hertz rules indicated the driver had to be at least 25 years old, sign a "no other driver" clause and promise not to race the vehicle. Before the last stipulation was added, GT350H models were showing up at rallies and racetracks for weekend events, spawning the term "rent-a-racer."

Hertz claimed that their repeat GT350 customers were often businessmen. Advance reservations were necessary since the cars were in selected areas

Louvers were removed from rear quarter windows in all GT350s for better visibility. Motor Trend magazine took the supercharged version through the quarter mile in 14 seconds at 102 mph with a Cruise-O-Matic transmission.

The Shelby grille was made up of horizontal bars. Bold racing stripes ran the length of the car.

The Cobra gas filler cap, located at the rear center, was a high-theft item.

Easy luggage access wasn't a ... of the hatchback bodice ...

The Shelby hood was latched with competition-style rings and pins.

Air scoops in the rear fenders were fully functional and used to ...

1966 Model Car Pricing

Falcon
4-door Sedan	$2,114
Futura 4-door Sedan	$2,237
Futura Station Wagon	$2,553

Fairlane
4-door Sedan I-6	$2,280
4-door Sedan V-8	$2,386

Fairlane 500
4-door Sedan I-6	$2,357
2-door Hardtop V-8	$2,484
Convertible V-8	$2,709
Squire Wagon V-8	$2,901

Fairlane 500XL
2-door Hardtop V-8	$2,649
GT Hardtop	$2,843
GT Convertible	$3,068

Custom
4-door Sedan I-6	$2,415
4-door Sedan V-8	$2,539

Custom 500
4-door Sedan I-6	$2,514
4-door Sedan V-8	$2,639

Galaxie 500
4-door Sedan I-6	$2,742
4-door Sedan V-8	$2,784

Galaxie 500XL
2-door Fastback	$3,208

Galaxie 500 7-Litre
2-door Fastback	$3,596
Convertible	$3,844

Galaxie 500 LTD
4-door Hardtop	$3,278

Mustang
Coupe I-6	$2,416
Convertible I-6	$2,653
Fastback I-6	$2,607

Station Wagons
Country Squire 9-pass. V-8	$3,292

Thunderbird
Coupe	$4,395
Town Hardtop	$4,451
Landau	$4,552

would demonstrate how well a Mustang would run even after the wear and tear of multiple drivers and high mileage.

Along with the Hertz production order, which started at 200 vehicles and quickly moved up to just under 1,000, Shelby was producing plenty of his GT350 models and a much smaller number of the Cobra 427 roadsters. This, plus running Ford's GT40 race team and working up prototypes of the 1967 GT350 and GT500 models, was keeping him more than busy. It was an exciting time at Shelby's California operation.

Ford Motor Company was an exciting place too, with the blue oval winning races across the United States and Europe and new products like Mustang defining segments of the buying public that no one knew existed. Although profits were becoming more of a challenge, Ford managed consistently to keep the company in the black for the shareholders. Henry II had made it clear, though, that the coming years would be tougher, with labor and material costs rising and government regulation becoming an immediate reality. Almost no one took notice of the 23,776 Bronco SUVs that began opening the sports utility market segment.

Mustang was still offered in convertible, coupe and fastback models. The hot GT option was available in any of the three body styles.

This Ford public relations photo shows Mustangs on an unrealistically tight time-trial course. (Photos this page: Ford Motor Company)

in limited numbers. The Detroit office carried 22 of the "H" models in both four-speed and automatic versions. Hertz and Ford also started a program to lend a GT350H to any legitimate journalist for two weeks free of charge for "road testing." This had to be done between July 15 and September 15, 1966. Ford felt this

1966 Shelby Mustang GT350

A Paxton supercharger was listed as an option on all Shelby GT350 models for an additional $670 over the base $4,428 price.

1966 Car Production

Fairlane
4-door Sedan	26,170
2-door Club Coupe	13,498

Fairlane 500
4-door Sedan	68,635
2-door Club Coupe	14,118
2-door Hardtop	75,947
Convertible	9,299

Fairlane 500XL
2-door Hardtop	23,942
Convertible	4,560

Fairlane GT
2-door Hardtop	33,015
Convertible	4,327

Fairlane Wagons
Ranch Wagon Custom	19,826
Ranch Wagon Standard	12,379
Squire Wagon	11,558

Falcon
4-door Sedan	34,685
2-door Club Coupe	41,432

Falcon Futura
4-door Sedan	34,039
2-door Club Coupe	21,997

Futura Sports Coupe
2-door, Bucket Seats	20,289

Falcon Ranchero
Standard	9,480
Deluxe	11,038
Deluxe, Bucket Seats	1,242

Falcon Wagons
4-door Standard	16,653
4-door Deluxe	13,574

Ford Custom
4-door Sedan	72,245
2-door Sedan	32,292

Ford Custom 500
4-door Sedan	109,449
2-door Sedan	28,789

Galaxie 500
4-door Sedan	171,886
4-door Fastback	54,884
2-door Fastback	198,532
Convertible	27,454

Galaxie 500 7-Litre
2-door Fastback	8,705
Convertible	2,368

Galaxie 500 LTD
4-door Fastback	69,400
2-door Fastback	31,696

Galaxie 500XL
2-door Fastback	25,715
Convertible	6,360

Mustang
2-door Fastback Standard	27,809
2-door Fastback Luxury	7,889
2-door Hardtop Standard	422,416
2-door Hardtop Luxury	55,938
2-door Hardtop, Bench Seats	21,397
Convertible	56,409
Convertible Luxury	12,520
Convertible, Bench Seats	3,190

Station Wagons
Ranch Wagon 6-passenger	33,306
Country Sedan 6-passenger	55,616
Country Sedan 10-passenger	36,633
Country Squire 6-passenger	27,645
Country Squire 10-passenger	41,953

Thunderbird
2-door Hardtop	13,389
2-door Town Hardtop	15,633
2-door Town Landau	35,105
Convertible	5,049
Total	**2,233,375**

The GT equipment group included dual exhaust, plated exhaust "trumpet" extensions, special handling package, front disc brakes, side racing stripes, GT fuel filler cap, black grille and special foglamps. (Photo: Ford Motor Company)

▶

Shelby's Mustangs became bigger and heavier. Ford wanted to see more luxury in them to try to boost sales volume.

FORD

Carroll Shelby's shop produced both GT350 and GT500 models for 1967. The new GT500 used the Ford 428 cubic inch V-8 producing 345 horsepower at 5,400 rpm.

The Year 1967

The auto business in the United States and Europe declined sharply in 1967 with depressed markets contributing to a disappointing year for Ford. Worldwide vehicle sales for Ford dropped to 3,588,592, down more than 900,000 units, and earnings for the company were down 86 percent. A two-month United Auto Workers strike in North America caused Ford to lose more than 600,000 units of production, adding to the losses. The strike started on September 7, when Ford was introducing its new models.

Trucks were now starting to become a major factor in company profits for North American manufacturers, with sales growing 70 percent from 1960 through the end of 1967. Ford was now the truck sales leader.

Based on retail sales, Ford was still the leading American manufacturer in Europe as it prepared to introduce the first Ford Escort the following year. Ford reorganized its automotive operations in Europe, Great Britain and northern Africa as Ford of Europe to better coordinate the company's activities there.

Henry Ford II continued his dedication to maintaining a well-balanced workforce. "We have gone a step beyond our long-established policy of nondiscriminatory hiring. We are now attempting to recruit and train as many so-called unemployables as our production needs and good business practice will permit. We believe that this is one practical means, consistent with our private enterprise system, for attacking poverty and other social ills at the roots."

The big news on who's who at Ford came with Henry II's hiring of Semon "Bunkie" Knudsen from General Motors as president of Ford Motor Company, replacing the retiring Arjay Miller. Knudsen's claim to fame at GM was his quick remaking of the Pontiac Division and its 1957 products. He had deleted the chrome hood stripes, revved up the engines and given the lackluster division a performance image. So Henry II figured his talents could be beneficial for Ford as well. Knudsen's father had left Ford to make something out of Chevrolet back in the 1920s, so history had come full circle.

Lee Iacocca made another big move up the corporate ladder, being named executive vice president of North American Automotive Operations, although he saw Knudsen's appointment as a setback to his career. Whiz kid Edward Lundy also became an executive vice president ruling over the finance world, and Ford Division General Manager Don Frey was promoted to vice president of the Product Development Group.

Products for 1967 now boasted more standard safety features, including thick-laminate safety glass windshields; front and rear seat belts; impact-absorbing steering assemblies; four-way emergency flashers; dual hydraulic brake systems; and padded instrument panels, sun visors and windshield pillars. These were all highlighted in advertising and press materials in hopes the government would see Ford as moving ahead willingly with safety improvements. Henry Ford II knew that if the manufacturers did not make progress on their own, the government would take the lead and make the rules for them. "We must be prepared to offer constructive alternatives to unwise legislation and administration, and we must work toward a climate in which constructive alternatives will be received with more sympathy," said Ford.

Showing more confidence in its new products, Ford Motor Company extended its power train warranty on all new Fords for 1967. Customers could now enjoy a 50,000-mile warranty on all engine, transmission and driveline parts of the vehicles. All other parts of the car still came with the standard 24,000-mile or two-year bumper-to-bumper warranty.

Ford

The full-size Fords were three inches longer this year and came in Custom, Galaxie, XL and LTD models. Standard on all big Fords were coil spring front and rear suspension, 15-inch tires, long-life battery, 240 cubic inch Big Six engine, fully synchronized three-speed manual transmission, two-speed wipers with washer and self-adjusting brakes.

All Ford models except the wagons traditionally were available with any engine. If you wanted to purchase a bottom-of-the-line Ford Custom with a 345 hp 428 V-8, four-speed transmission and locking differential, you could have an economically priced street racer. Option packages were not yet the standard, and you could tailor your Ford to suit your needs and budget.

Optional V-8 engines for the Ford were a 200 hp 289 V-8, 270 and 315 hp 390 V-8s and the top-of-the-line 428 V-8 producing 345 hp. You could still order Cruise-O-Matic with any engine and a four-speed with either the 390 or 428 V-8. The 427 V-8 engine was technically available but was really a competition engine and not practical for the street. The 428 V-8 was much less expensive to build and easier on warranty costs for the company.

A Galaxie 500XL hardtop weighed in at 3,770 pounds and the convertible moved up to 3,970, so the Big Six wasn't a viable

option for moving them around town or down the highway. The XL models came standard with a 200 hp Challenger 289 V-8, and Ford dealers encouraged buyers to upgrade to the optional 390 at either 270 or 315 hp. The XL 7-Litre package added the 428 V-8, dual exhausts, power front disc brakes, Wide-Oval tires and a simulated wood steering wheel.

The Galaxie 500 two-door hardtop was the big seller, moving more than 197,000 units in 1967. (Photo: Ford Motor Company)

Ford's Big Six had trouble moving the 3,770-pound Ford hardtop around, so the XL models came with a standard 200 hp Challenger 289 V-8. The 390 V-8 was a common option, offering 270 or 315 hp, enough to move either the hardtop or heavier convertible down the road with ease.

Optional V-8 engines for the Ford were a 200 hp 289 V-8, 270 and 315 hp 390 V-8s and the top-of-the-line 428 V-8 producing 345 hp.

The 1967 Falcon changed little, having been restyled the previous year, and sales dropped by more than 135,000 units. (Photos this page: Ford Motor Company)

The Galaxie 500 four-door sedan and two-door hardtop models were the big sellers for Ford. Both provided a combination of luxury, sportiness and value that the buyer wanted, and the sales of these two models totaled almost 330,000 units. All Galaxie 500 models carried a 25-gallon fuel tank and provided 19.1 cubic feet of luggage space. For around $2,800 you could have a Galaxie 500 two-door hardtop with whitewall tires, full wheel covers and a Super Diamond Lustre Enamel paint job. A well-equipped XL model with a 270 hp 390 V-8, whitewall tires and vinyl roof was $3,482.

1967 Ford Options

345 hp 428 V-8	351.49
Limited slip differential	41.60
7-Litre sports package	515.86
Power windows	99.94
SelectAire conditioner	356.09
Full tinted glass	39.45
Speed control	71.30
AM radio w/Stereo-Sonic Tape	128.49
Rear seat speaker	13.22
AM/FM radio	133.65

Falcon

Having been completely restyled the previous year, the new Falcon was changed little for 1967. Sales took a complete nosedive, from more than 200,000 in 1966 to a meager 64,335 in 1967. There was tougher competition from other manufacturers, but the most likely reason for the drop was that Fairlane, a car too similar in size and value, was cannibalizing it. Instead of bringing in new buyers from competitors, Fairlane was bringing in Falcon owners wanting to upgrade, as Ford was finding out.

Falcon received the 225 hp 289 V-8 option, adding a respectable amount of power to an otherwise mundane car. Other engines were the standard 170 and the 200 cubic inch I-6 power plants or the 200 hp 289 V-8. Cruise-O-Matic or four-speed manual transmissions were optional.

Falcon was practical, with its 12 cubic feet of luggage space, fuel efficiency and roomy interior. SelectAire conditioning was now

integrated into the dash and an optional Stereo-Sonic Tape System made Falcon owners feel like they were riding in a value-priced luxury car. Mustang had quickly displaced the previous, sporty Falcon Sprints considering its looks and low cost. Falcon had become a value-priced, ordinary little car that could see its end in sight.

1967 Falcon Options

225 hp 289 V-8	156.71
Limited slip differential	37.20
Full tinted glass	30.73
Vinyl roof	74.19
Stereo-Sonic Tape System	128.49
Whitewall tires	32.47
Wheel covers	21.34
Push-button AM radio	57.44

Fairlane

Sales of the Fairlane were substantially short of the 1966 model year sales. Changes were minor for 1967. The basic body was untouched but the grille was changed from a single horizontal bar to a bar with three vertical chrome strips and a Ford crest in the center. Fairlanes carried standard highlights such as a 20-gallon fuel tank, 15.2 cubic feet of luggage space, a reversible key and a 50,000-mile power train warranty.

Ordering a GT or GT/A model automatically upgraded the Fairlane to a Challenger 289 V-8 with 200 hp, front disc brakes, deep cushioned bucket seats, Wide-Oval tires and deluxe wheel covers. Two optional 390 V-8s with 270 and 320 hp were offered at extra cost. This was quite different from the previous year when the newly introduced Fairlane GT came with a 335 hp 390 V-8.

Fairlanes below the GT level came standard with a 120 hp 200 I-6. Optional on all models was a 200 hp 289 V-8 or a 390 V-8 rated at 270 hp with a two-barrel carburetor or the 270 or 320

The Fairlane 500 convertible with a V-8 started at $2,770.

GT and GT/A models came standard with a Challenger 289 V-8 with 200 hp, front disc brakes, deep cushioned bucket seats, Wide-Oval tires and deluxe wheel covers. The 270 and 320 hp 390 V-8s were extra-cost options. (Photos this page: Ford Motor Company)

All-new for '67:
Fairlane Ranchero with Thunderbird thunder.

Right from the first look you know something wonderful's happened to Ranchero. It's longer, leaner, with all the promise of excitement you'd expect in a Fairlane. And how Ranchero delivers on that promise! It begins with an optional 390-cubic-inch Thunderbird V-8 — just one of four engines available. Add a fully synchronized four-speed transmission with floor shift — or SelectShift Cruise-O-Matic, that gives you the convenience and the fun of both manual and completely automatic shifting. Complete the picture with individually adjustable, contoured bucket seats, center console, radio/stereo-sonic tape system, and air conditioning. And for the greatest thrill, check Ranchero's price tag. It's the one thing about this beauty that's not big, bold and luxurious. **Fairlane Ranchero/67**

Go automatic – or shift for yourself. New optional SelectShift Cruise-O-Matic allows you to do both • Center: handsome interior of Fairlane Ranchero 500XL, one of three models available • Roomy 6½ foot box with double wall sides for added strength, one hand tailgate latch for easy operation. Overall Ranchero load capacity now up to 1250 pounds.

You're ahead in a Ford.

With much sportier body styling and room for a bigger V-8, Ranchero became a part of the Fairlane family, leaving Falcon with a shrinking model lineup.

hp versions with a four-barrel. SelectShift Cruise-O-Matic was available with all engines and a four-speed could be mated to any V-8.

While there was actually a 427 cubic inch (side-oiler) engine available for order in both 1966 and 1967, it was an extremely expensive option for a mid-1960s car at $1,129. Added to the production options list to homologate it for racing, it wasn't exactly practical for street use. The big block, different from the 1963–64 top-oiler 427 engine, came with a shortened three month power train warranty

because Ford expected the engine to be run hard, and strongly suggested that it not be driven on the street. Buyers had to sign a disclaimer at the dealership before the order would be placed. "In a continuing effort to satisfy every demand of its customers, Ford Division of Ford Motor Company is now producing special high performance cars and components designed exclusively for use in supervised competitive events. These special vehicles and components are not intended for highway or general passenger car use." Even Ford sales literature warned, "Limited production

engines. Available only for special purchase."

Ranchero became a part of the Fairlane family this year, moving away from Falcon and into the true mid-size family. With much sportier body styling and room for a bigger block, Ranchero became a car with a performance following. It was for those wanting something with the comfort and performance attributes of a car but capable of hauling light cargo. Above the standard 200 cubic inch inline six there were two 289 V-8 options with 200 and 225 hp. Cruise-O-Matic or four-speed transmissions were available for either V-8.

1967 Fairlane Options

320 hp 390 V-8	263.71
Cruise-O-Matic	220.17
4-speed manual transmission	184.02
Power front disc brakes	42.29
Full tinted glass	30.73
Power steering	84.47
Center console	47.92
Power convertible top	52.95
Vinyl roof	74.36
SelectAire conditioner	356.09

Thunderbird

Ford marketing made a conscious decision early on to move Thunderbird from a two-seater to a more upscale vehicle. The company knew that the two-seat 1955–57 Thunderbird was cute and had been good for the Ford image but provided little help with volume sales and profits. This was proven, much to the chagrin of the classic T-Bird fans, when production jumped from 21,380 in 1957 to 67,456 in 1959, the second year of the four-seater. Encouraged by the customer response to its making the vehicle larger and more luxurious, Ford continued to move up the ladder and in 1967 introduced the largest and heaviest T-Bird to date.

With Thunderbird in its 13th year, Ford wanted to make a big splash for its newest version

Thunderbird was in its 13th year and had grown into a heavy sports luxury sedan with no resemblance to its roots.

Thunderbird's hidden headlamps were powered by engine vacuum and could also be manually operated with a hand crank. (Photos this page: Ford Motor Company)

of the personal luxury model. Introducing the first four-door Thunderbird gave Ford something to hype and advertise. Thunderbird now shared with its Lincoln Continental cousin the suicide-door format, with all doors opening from the B-pillar. The exterior styling included hidden headlamps mounted in the grille, the new four-door

configuration in Landau trim and a full-width taillight look above the flush-mounted chrome rear bumper. The hidden headlamps were powered by engine vacuum and could be manually operated if necessary.

The T-Bird interior was full of simulated wood grain on the dashboard; a tilt steering wheel; tufted upholstery in cloth, vinyl or

leather; and a center console that flowed down from the dash and between the front seats. Adjustable front bucket seats were standard but, surprisingly enough, air conditioning was still an option.

There were plenty of options for Thunderbird to help drive the price up and make it even more luxurious. Adding the SelectAire conditioner tagged $421 on to the price, and other optional equipment included power windows, six-way power driver's seat, tinted glass, front shoulder harness, AM radio with Stereo-Sonic Tape System and two-tone paint.

Standard Thunderbird power for all models came from the 315 hp 390 V-8, and for an additional $90 you could have the 345 hp 428 V-8. Although the 428 V-8 provided an increase of only 30 horsepower it moved up from 427 ft.-lbs. of torque to 462 ft.-lbs. at 2,800 rpm.

SelectShift Cruise-O-Matic transmission came standard and a limited slip differential was still on the option list for an additional $46.

1967 Thunderbird Options

345 hp 428 V-8	90.68
Power antenna	28.97
6-way power driver's seat	97.32
Power trunk lid release	12.63
Power windows	103.95
Limited slip differential	46.69
SelectAire conditioner	421.49
Convenience control panel 2-door	77.73
Cruise control	129.55
Tinted Glass	47.49
AM/FM radio	89.94
Two-tone paint	25.25

Mustang

"Ponies for Sale" read the headline. Motorized Mustang model cars were being offered for $5.50 in *Ford World* advertisements for the 1966 hardtop and 1967 2+2. The battery-powered cars would go forward or backward and had wheels that would turn.

This was only one example of how Mustang mania had driven marketing in new directions.

Ford Mustang for 1967 featured a new body style for the convertible, coupe and fastback. All V-8 models were available with SelectShift Cruise-O-Matic for automatic or manual shifting. The power train, suspension and steering warranty from Ford was now five years or 50,000 miles, while the bumper-to-bumper warranty stayed at three years or 36,000 miles.

The GT Equipment Group provided a great performance value at $205.05. It included either a 271 horsepower 289 V-8 or the 320 horsepower 390 V-8, power front disc brakes, foglamps, dual exhausts and Firestone Wide-Oval tires. (Photos this page: Ford Motor Company)

Ford's Mustang GT/A constituted a GT package with an automatic transmission. The package could be added to any of the three models.

The 1967 Mustang had competition from Chevrolet's new Camaro, also sitting on a 108-inch wheelbase but with less horsepower.

There were Mustang jackets, children's pedal cars and plastic model car kits all being sold or used as promotions for the Mustang. Not only did these promotions help to keep the profile of the new car flying high, they also brought in extra profits for dealers and other companies.

The 1967 Mustang brought the first styling change for the overnight success story. It was billed as having "a longer, wider look and a wider tread for better road grip." The new hardtop model was 141 pounds heavier and $63.03 more costly than the comparable 1966. The price increases were kept to a mini-mum, and the extra weight was all in the chassis and body since the same engine was still standard.

The GT with a 390 V-8 (pictured) kicked out 320 hp or with the smaller 289 V-8, 271 hp.

The GT500 models had plenty of torque and an extra 176 pounds of front-end weight over the GT350 model, causing heavy understeer.

By 1967 there were already more than one million editions of Mustangs on highways, mostly in North America with a few scattered across Europe and Australia. Even though it had an entirely new body, Mustang continued with the same basic styling cues as the original model. It still came in a coupe, convertible and 2+2, which came with an even more sloped fastback roofline traveling to the very back of the deck lid. The car was now two inches longer and 2.7 inches wider.

The rear taillights were made up of three small vertical lights on either side, separated by approximately an inch of sheet metal. The hood on the GT model had two non-functioning air vents.

Inside, the new Mustangs were substantially different. The seats now used softer vinyl upholstery and the dash was completely redesigned with an integrated air conditioning system. The earlier models had the air conditioning hanging below the dash, blocking part of the floor space. The optional tachometer was dropped into the instrument panel instead of being mounted on the steering column as it had been with the Rally Pac option. Having the tach in the dash displaced the oil pressure and alternator gauges, turning these two important gauges into idiot lights. The 2+2 rear seat was

fixed in place in the new design but a fold-down version could be ordered at extra cost. A tilt and swing-away steering column was also optional for 1967.

Although the suspension in the new models was similar to that in previous Mustangs, the tread was now two inches wider across the front, providing more under-hood room for the new 390 V-8. With longer, modified A-arms, the turning diameter was shortened by five feet and the steering was more responsive. Mustang, originally built mostly from Falcon parts, was now sharing many suspension parts with the bigger Fairlane and current Falcon.

Among the changes were lowering the A-arm pivot to raise the front roll center. Apparently Ford borrowed this technique from the Shelby GT350 to help keep the outside front wheel perpendicular to the road during hard cornering. This provided more road-gripping contact with the pavement and a better handling chassis overall than earlier Mustangs.

If you ordered the GT sports package, a Competition Handling Package was also available at additional cost. The handling package came with stiffer springs, larger stabilizer bar, Koni shocks and Firestone Wide-Oval tires. It made a great road racer out of the Mustang, although it was hard on the kidneys for everyday usage.

1967 Model Car Pricing

Falcon

4-door Sedan	$2,167
Futura Sports Coupe	$2,280
Futura Squire Wagon	$2,609

Fairlane

4-door Sedan I-6	$2,339
4-door Sedan V-8	$2,445

Fairlane 500

4-door Sedan V-8	$2,522
Hardtop Coupe V-8	$2,545
Convertible V-8	$2,770
Squire Wagon V-8	$3,007

Fairlane 500XL

2-door Hardtop V-8	$2,724
GT Hardtop	$2,839
GT Convertible	$3,064

Custom

4-door Sedan I-6	$2,496
4-door Sedan V-8	$2,602

Custom 500

4-door Sedan V-8	$2,701

Galaxie 500

4-door Sedan I-6	$2,732
4-door Sedan V-8	$2,838

Galaxie 500XL

2-door Fastback Coupe	$3,243
Convertible	$3,493

LTD

4-door Sedan	$3,298
2-door Hardtop Coupe	$3,362

Mustang

Coupe I-6	$2,461
Convertible I-6	$2,698
Fastback I-6	$2,592

Station Wagons

Country Squire 9-passenger	$3,466

Thunderbird

Coupe	$4,603
Landau 2-door	$4,704
Landau 4-door	$4,825

Air conditioning, power steering and brakes were installed on the GT500 model as it changed into a sports luxury machine.

The Shelby Mustangs were fitted with their own fiberglass nosepieces giving them a distinctive look. The GT500 model came with grille-mounted driving lights and a 7-litre Ford power plant.

Although the GT500 had plenty of horsepower and torque, it also carried a heavy weight penalty at the front of the vehicle. The GT350 model with its lighter power plant handled

Interiors were outfitted with ribbed vinyl bucket seats with a Cobra emblem stamped in the seatback.

The pillar-mounted side scoops drafted air from the interior while the rear fender-mounted scoops brought cool air to vent the rear brakes.

1967 Shelby Mustang GT500

For 1967 the new model Shelby GT500 production was 2,048 units and
that for the GT350 models only 1,175.

The Mach I concept definitely gave the public a peek at things to come. Although a concept, the Mach I had all the styling cues of the new production-model Mustang.

The Mach 1 profile was a close match to its production namesake. Ford wanted to get public reaction to the concept by showing it at auto shows and getting it published in magazines.

The Cobra show car had some early GT40 in it and had little to do with the Shelby Cobra Styling. This particular vehicle had no engine or interior and was used strictly as an internal design study. (Photos this page: Ford Motor Company)

Ford Engines for 1967			
CID	Carb.	Comp.	HP
170 I-6	1 bbl	9.1	105 @ 4400
200 I-6	1 bbl	9.2	120 @ 4400
240 I-6	1 bbl	9.2	150 @ 4200
289 V-8	2 bbl	9.3	200 @ 4400
289 V-8	4 bbl	10.0	225 @ 4800
289 V-8	4 bbl	10.5	271 @ 6000
390 V-8	2 bbl	9.5	270 @ 4400
390 V-8	4 bbl	10.5	315 @ 4600
390 V-8	4 bbl	10.5	320 @ 4600
428 V-8	4 bbl	10.5	345 @ 5400

Engine choices continued to be the standard 120 hp 200 I-6, two versions of the 289 V-8 (225 hp or 271 hp) and the new 320 hp 390 V-8 found in the Fairlane GT and GT/A. Transmissions were fully synchronized three- or four-speeds or the SelectShift Cruise-O-Matic. This was the same automatic found on the Fairlane GT/A. Road tests on the GT/A version of the 390 Mustang recorded zero-to-60 mph times of 7.4 seconds and 94 mph in the quarter mile.

Ford now gave Mustang convertible buyers the option of a standard plastic backlight or an optional hinged glass backlight that folded in half when the roof was in the down position. This was a big improvement for convertible owners, who could now worry a little less about leaving their cars out in inclement weather.

With many new improvements, Mustang was still selling like hotcakes and was actually a much-improved car. The sales were still excellent and both the GM and Chrysler entries were far behind the pony car in all respects.

1967 Mustang Options

320 hp 390 V-8	263.71
Cruise-O-Matic	220.17
4-speed manual transmission	233.18
Power front disc brakes	64.77
Power steering	84.47
Power convertible top	52.95
Tilt-away steering wheel	59.93
Stereo-Sonic Tape System	128.49
Full-width front seat	24.42
SelectAire conditioner	356.09
2+2 folding rear seat, fastback	64.77
GT equipment group	151.10

With a Talladega-like fastback, the Ford Magic Cruiser could be a sporty ride for Dad during the week and a station wagon for the family on weekends. A two-person, rear-facing seat popped up out of the trunk floor to create an eight-passenger vehicle within seconds. (Photos this page: Ford Motor Company)

1967 Car Production

Fairlane
4-door	19,740
2-door	10,628

Fairlane 500
4-door	51,552
2-door Club Coupe	8,473
2-door Hardtop	70,135
Convertible	5,428

Fairlane 500XL
2-door Hardtop, Bucket Seats	14,871
Convertible, Bucket Seats	1,943

Fairlane Ranchero
Standard	5,858
500	9,504
500XL	1,881

Fairlane GT
2-door Hardtop, Bucket Seats	18,670
Convertible, Bucket Seats	2,117

Falcon
4-door	13,554
2-door	16,082

Falcon Futura
4-door	11,254
2-door Club Coupe	6,287
Sports Coupe, Bucket Seats	7,053

Falcon Wagons
Standard	5,553
Futura	4,552

Ford Custom
4-door	41,417
2-door	18,107

Ford Custom 500
4-door	83,260
2-door	18,146

Ford LTD
4-door	12,491
4-door Hardtop, Bucket Seats	51,978
2-door Hardtop, Bucket Seats	46,036

Galaxie 500
4-door	130,063
4-door Hardtop	57,087
2-door Hardtop	197,388
Convertible	19,068

Galaxie 500XL
2-door Hardtop, Bucket Seats	18,174
Convertible, Bucket Seats	5,161

Mustang
2-door Fastback	53,651
2-door Fastback Luxury	17,391
2-door Hardtop	325,853
2-door Hardtop Luxury	22,228
2-door Hardtop, Bench Seats	8,190
Convertible	38,751
Convertible Luxury	4,848
Convertible, Bench Seats	1,209

Station Wagons
Country Squire	8,348
Country Squire 6-passenger	25,600
Country Squire 10-passenger	44,024
Country Sedan 6-passenger	50,818
Country Sedan 10-passenger	34,377
Ranch Wagon	10,881
Ranch Wagon 6-passenger	23,932
Custom Ranch Wagon	15,902

Thunderbird
4-door Hardtop Landau	24,967
2-door Hardtop	15,567
2-door Hardtop Landau	37,422
Total	**1,747,470**

Shelby Mustangs

With the introduction of the all-new 1967 Mustang, Shelby American had to work up new designs to build in the California facility. Ford Motor Company assigned one of their designers, Chuck McHose, to Shelby to work out the new body design and modifications. Ford wanted to see more luxury and options in the new cars to increase sales, so two versions were built: a GT350 with the 289 V-8 and a GT500 with a big-block Ford 428 engine.

Shelby talked about the decision to build a big-block version of the Mustang instead of staying exclusively with the GT350. "The GT500 came about because to get our volume up to the projected 5,000 we hoped for, we realized we had to put on power steering, air conditioning and a lot of other features that were necessary to sell more cars. Back in 1966, we sold barely enough cars to break even. The larger engine was necessary to pull all this equipment and still give some performance."

Three 427 V-8 powered GT500s were produced in 1967. Two were built with the standard 427 side-oiler engine and one was specially built with a 427 lightweight engine as an engineering study, VIN# 67402F4A00544. It had a GT40 MK II engine, competition headers and aluminum heads. Dubbed the "Super Snake," it was driven by Carroll Shelby at Goodyear's San Angelo, Texas, test track at speeds up to 170 mph as he gave rides to press members from *Time* and *Life* magazines. Shelby American's chief engineer Fred Goodell then drove it around the track for 500 miles at an average speed of 142 miles per hour!

Shelby American was looking to unload the Super Snake one-off fastback and approached Don McCain, who had been the Shelby American field sales representative and driving force behind the GT350 drag racing program. McCain had moved on to a new job as the high-performance sales manager for Mel Burns Ford in Long Beach, California. It was McCain who first came up with the idea of building a limited run of 50 Super Snakes that would be sold only through Mel Burns Ford. But when he figured out that it would have to retail at $7,500, he knew it would never sell as you could buy a 427 Cobra for about the same price. So the only Super Snake was sold to two airline pilots, James Gorman and James Hadden, who set it up for drag racing. The invoice indicated they used the Braniff Credit Union to finance the vehicle.

▶

The 1968 Shelby Mustangs were available in either GT350 or GT500 trim. (Photo: Ford Motor Company)

FORD

The Year 1968

The big Shelby GT500 models were now in full swing, with plenty of straight-line power. The Shelby Mustangs were now being built by the A. O. Smith Company in Ionia, Michigan.

It wasn't business as usual for Ford Motor Company in 1968. Ford sold 4.7 million vehicles, a million plus more than in strike-laden 1967. Between 1960 and 1968, total industry sales in the United States had increased from six million vehicles per year to more than nine million—a 50 percent gain. Ford Division truck sales broke all previous records and allowed Ford to retain its truck sales leadership established in 1967. In Europe the one-year-old Escort was also a success and the first car to be built by both Ford of Germany and Ford of Britain. Ford was also watching sales trends showing that customers were buying more options and higher levels of car models. That could translate into higher profits for each vehicle sold, so Ford started pushing more options in sales brochures.

Apparently automotive dealer service for the industry, including warranty service, wasn't up to par and was the subject of Washington hearings in 1968. Henry II pointed out to stockholders that many of these problems were coming as annual production rose and complexity of the vehicles increased. Because customer loyalty depended on satisfaction with service after the sale, Henry II laid out a three-part program to improve the situation.

First, he instituted a new program to design future cars and trucks for quicker, easier completion of the most often performed service tasks. Second, Ford would increase the service intervals for new vehicles by improving manufacturing quality and designing in more reliability. And third, the company would institute programs to help the dealers expand the service areas, improve the level of service equipment, and recruit and train new mechanics.

Ford met the government's industry challenge to reduce engine emissions, reducing hydrocarbons and carbon monoxide by almost 60 percent compared to 1960 levels. Safety features were still confined to the deep-dish steering wheel, padded dash and windshield pillars, safety belts and less protruding knobs and buttons in the dash area.

Ford

Styling changes on the 1968 full-size Fords included full-width front grille that held retractable headlamps on the LTD and XL models. Minor trim changes included Ford block letters on the right side of the deck lid, a flatter mesh front grille for the non-LTD and XL models and lower front fenders to accommodate the return to horizontal headlamps.

A January 1968 *Car Life* magazine road test of the XL

While plenty of engine power options were available for the big Fords, handling was not a strong suit. (Photo: Ford Motor Company)

428 Fastback noted, "Straight line performance is more than adequate, whether the criteria be acceleration or top speed. Economy should not be a primary concern in selecting such a car, at least with a 428-CID engine, but the XL consistently delivered 11 to 12 mpg in very vigorous driving." The road test revealed a car that was a wonderful cruiser while lacking any good handling characteristics, which was probably to be expected considering the weight of the engine and overall size of the vehicle. Top speed was 123 mph at 4,450 rpm and zero-to-60 mph time was 8.2 seconds. The 428 V-8 was relatively inexpensive to build and provided plenty of torque and adequate acceleration with low warranty costs for Ford.

While engines for the big Fords continued to evolve at the upper end, the 150 hp 240 cubic inch inline-six was standard on all models below the LTD. Optional engines for all Ford two- and four-door models were the 210 hp 302 V-8 (standard on LTD and Country Squire), 230 hp 302 V-8, 265 hp 390 V-8, 315 hp 390 V-8, 390 hp 427 V-8 and 340 hp 428 V-8 power plants.

1968 Ford Options

340 hp 428 V-8	244.47
Power windows	99.94
SelectAire conditioner	368.72
Full tinted glass	47.49
Speed control	97.91
Front shoulder belts	23.38
AM radio w/Stereo-Sonic Tape	128.49
Tilt-away steering wheel	66.14
Power antenna	28.97
Limited slip differential	46.69
Rear window defogger	21.27

Falcon

Offered in Falcon and Falcon Futura models, Ford's compact was similar to the previous year's

model, but offered a hot 230 hp 302 V-8, and sales shot up to 131,389, more than double the 1967 volume.

The body style stayed much the same, with small enhancements and changes such as a new split grille and a front bumper with a slotted air intake to improved engine cooling. The rear quarter panels and taillights took on a squarer design than before. The Falcon interior now had a more heavily padded instrument panel and lighted ignition switch and heater and air conditioning controls.

The base engine was still the 170 cubic inch I-6, with a

The big Fords returned to horizontal headlamps for 1968, which also allowed for lower front fenders. (Photo: Ford Motor Company)

LTD and XL models came standard with a full-width grille across the front of the car that held retractable headlamps. The fastback sloping roofline flowed most of the way to the rear of the car. (Photos this page: Ford Motor Company)

200 cubic inch I-6 upgrade available. The 289 V-8 was rated at 195 hp for the Falcon and the top-of-the-line power for 1968 was the 302 four-barrel V-8 with 230 hp.

1968 Falcon Options

230 hp 302 V-8	197.68
Full tinted glass	30.73
Vinyl roof	74.19
AM/FM stereo radio	181.36
Front shoulder belts	23.38
Rear window defogger	21.27
Sport wheel covers	34.29
Heavy-duty suspension (wagons)	23.38
Limited slip differential	41.60

Fairlane/Torino

Ford was walking a tightrope with its total model lineup, trying to keep the Ford, Falcon, Fairlane, Mustang and Thunderbird models different enough to cover all types of buyers. Mustang and Thunderbird fell within clearly defined segments and were not an issue. The main problem was with Falcon, Fairlane/Torino and the full-size Ford. The sizes were getting closer and so were the sticker prices. To save production and development costs, Falcon and Fairlane were built on the same platform, leaving the customer to wonder why they would want a Falcon when for $163 more they could have the stylish new Fairlane. The base Ford Custom sedan was only $178 above the base Fairlane, but none of this seemed to slow sales. Ford still had an amazing year in all three segments, producing 867,292 big Fords, 131,389 Falcons and 389,039 Fairlane/Torinos. Fairlane sales were up more than 100,000 over the previous year.

The big news for 1968 was the sporty Torino, an all-new upscale Fairlane series. Torino added six new models that hit both the luxury and sports interests of potential buyers. This was an important addition to help Ford boost the flagging Fairlane image. Fairlane was still selling well but not at levels the company had hoped for. The Torino addition would give Ford broader sales potential, providing models ranging from a base family sedan to a drag strip–ready rubber burner.

Torino was simply an extension of the Fairlane line, just above the Fairlane 500 models. The non-GT came in a two-door hardtop or four-door sedan while the GT models came in a two-door hardtop, two-door fastback or a convertible. Ford wanted the entire lineup to reflect a sporty, youthful look so deleted the two-door sedan from the entire lineup. All two-door hardtops eliminated the traditional vent window. Styling on the new Fairlane/Torino emphasized the long hood and short rear deck look that was so successful with Mustang. Overall length of the Torino and Fairlane was now four inches longer than for previous models.

All-new options on Fairlane and Torino models included power side windows, dual rear speakers for the AM radio, push-button memory positions for the AM/FM radio and warning lights to indicate door ajar, low fuel, parking brake on and seat belts unfastened. A rear defogger was available for all models except the wagon and convertible. The convertible models now came with a hidden clip-type boot fastener that gave a clean, smooth appearance with the top down. Interiors for all new models featured a Comfort Ventilation system that provided a stream of air to the interior with all windows closed.

Torino GT models came standard with a 210 hp 302 V-8 engine while all other Fairlane/Torino models came equipped with a 115 hp 200 I-6 power plant. Optional engines on all models were the 210 hp 302 V-8, 265 hp 390 V-8 and the 325 hp 390 V-8. Ford offered a Cobra 427 engine with a four-barrel carburetor early in production. The 427 V-8 developed 390 hp and could be matched with Ford's SelectShift Cruise-O-Matic transmission or a three- or four- speed manual.

Torino, the upscale Fairlane series, was chosen as the Indianapolis 500 pace car, driven by William Clay Ford.

Torino GT models came standard with a 210 hp 302 V-8 engine. The graceful fastback roofline made the Torino the logical choice for NASCAR racing.

All Fairlane/Torino models, except the wagon and convertible, were now available with a rear defogger. Power side windows, dual rear speakers for the AM radio and push-button memory positions for the AM/FM radio were also optional. (Photos this page: Ford Motor Company)

Ranchero became a full-fledged Fairlane in 1968, now using the new Fairlane body panels, chassis and engine combinations.

The Ranchero provided a carlike ride, great performance and a cargo area for light hauling.

The Fairlane wagon was popular, because the price was great and the mid-size platform provided plenty of room inside. (Photos this page: Ford Motor Company)

By mid-1968, both Fairlane and Mustang increased pressure on the competition by adding the 428 Cobra Jet V-8 to the options list. The conservatively rated 335 hp Cobra Jet came with a 10.6:1 compression ratio and put out 440 ft.-lbs. of torque at a low 3,400 rpm. The Cobra Jet option was an extra $306.27 over the base V-8 for the Fairlane and was not available on any of the wagon models.

Pace cars for Indianapolis had been a hot promotional tool for manufacturers introducing sporty new models. Ford had padded the race on a number of occasions with a "Ford" at the wheel. Henry II had driven a Lincoln V-12 in 1946, William Clay Ford drove his first event in 1953 in a Sunliner, and younger brother Benson drove the new Mustang in 1964 and a Mercury Comet Cyclone GT in 1966. Manufacturers had to pay a very hefty fee to have their car "chosen" to lead the field of open wheel racers. With the new Fairlane/Torino critical to Ford's sales success, a Torino convertible was named to pace the 1968 Indy event with William Clay taking his second turn at the wheel.

1968 Fairlane/Torino Options

390 hp 427 V-8	622.97
Cruise-O-Matic w/427 V-8	233.17
Limited slip differential	41.60
Power front disc brakes	64.77
Full tinted glass	34.97
Power steering	94.95
Power windows	99.94
Front shoulder belts	23.38
Vinyl roof	84.99
SelectAire conditioner	360.30

Thunderbird

Ford Thunderbird body styling for 1968 was mostly a carryover from the previous year. Minor exterior changes included a chrome grille with widely spaced horizontal and vertical chrome bars. The headlamps were still retractable, with a small Thunderbird emblem showing on each when closed.

Thunderbird styling was basically carried over for 1968.

Buyers had the choice of two-door hardtop, two-door Landau or four-door Landau models.

Ford released an engine option for Thunderbird in 1968, the new 429 Thunder Jet V-8 producing 360 horsepower.

The front bumper was freshened to show chrome on the upper edge with body-color paint on the lower portion. Ford added a wide center slot to provide more air for the new big-block optional engine.

The interior did receive some changes to increase room and comfort for Thunderbird buyers. The passenger capacity was moved from five to six because of the standard "Flight Bench" seat

Interior space was changed to provide more space and comfort for the occupants. (Photos this page: Ford Motor Company)

(bucket seats were still available at extra cost), more shoulder- and legroom was added, the transmission housing "hump" was lowered, and the floors were lower and flatter than in 1967.

Body styles came in a two-door hardtop, two-door Landau or four-door Landau. The Landau model was still the top Thunderbird and was easily noticed by the standard vinyl roof with the chrome "S" Landau Bar across the C-pillar. The new Flight Bench seat came with a fold-down armrest. If you ordered the optional bucket seats, you also had to pay extra for the floor-mounted console. The console had a lockable storage compartment and there was also space for four eight-track tapes in the forward storage compartment.

The standard engine was the 390 V-8 with 315 horsepower, and the optional engine was Ford's all-new 429 Thunder Jet V-8 producing 360 horsepower. The 429 V-8 was the first Ford engine to have any emissions controls engineered into the engine design. Both engines came standard with low-restriction dual exhaust systems. The automatic SelectShift Cruise-O-Matic was the only transmission available for Thunderbird.

Options still included the extra-cost power windows while power steering and brakes were now standard. An AM radio was also standard, or for a few dollars more, an AM/FM stereo radio and Stereo-Sonic Tape System were available. Other extra-cost options were the leather and vinyl interior, tilt-away steering wheel, speed control and an "alligator-grain" vinyl roof.

Horsepower and weight were both on the increase in the Ford lineup, as the vehicles all got bigger. Emissions equipment was becoming more important to all the manufacturers as the government closed in with new rules and deadlines, and Ford was hustling to meet the standards without losing the horsepower race. Nineteen sixty-nine was certain to be an interesting year.

1968 Thunderbird Options

360 hp 429 V-8	53.18
SelectShift Cruise-O-Matic	standard
Power windows	103.95
SelectAire w/Climate Control	499.22
6-way power seat	97.32
AM radio w/Stereo-Sonic Tape	128.49
Front shoulder belts	23.38
Tilt-away steering wheel	66.14
Power deck lid release	13.69
4-note horn	15.59
Front cornering lights	33.70

Mustang

The 1968 Mustang body styling stayed very close to the recently redesigned 1967 model, continuing with the hardtop, convertible and 2+2 fastback.

The GT package was similar to that of previous years and could be added to any V-8 powered Mustang. The package included heavy-duty suspension with high-rate front and rear springs, higher capacity shocks, larger diameter stabilizer bar, low-restriction exhausts, Wide-Oval tires, six-inch wheel rims, foglights and a GT flip-open gas cap. The GT package was an extra $146.

Other options included AM/FM stereo radio, full-width front seat, speed control, SelectShift Cruise-O-Matic, eight-track Stereo-Sonic Tape System, four-speed manual transmission, tilt-away steering wheel and SelectAire conditioning.

Engines for the 1968 models started with the basic 115 horsepower 200 cubic inch six and moved all the way up to a 335 horsepower 428 cubic inch V-8.

Mustang, like Fairlane, received the new high-performance 428 Cobra Jet V-8 as a 1968½ model. Ford favored April introductions to keep the competition off balance and ship exciting new midyear products to its dealers.

The Mustang could be identified by the fiberglass "power dome" on the hood (the Fairlane hood stayed unchanged) and a black stripe that extended from the front of the hood to the base of the windshield. The option price of the 335 hp Mustang Cobra Jet with the Ram Air system was $420 over the base V-8.

1968 Mustang Options

390 hp 427 V-8	622.97
325 hp 390 V-8	158.08
Cruise-O-Matic w/427 V-8	233.17
Power front disc brakes	64.77
Power steering	84.47
Power convertible top	52.95
Tilt-away steering wheel	66.14
Stereo-Sonic Tape System	133.86
Full-width front seat	32.44
Front shoulder belts	23.38
Vinyl roof	64.77

The base 1968 Mustang hardtop was by far the best-selling model, accounting for 233,472 of total Mustang production. (Photo: Ford Motor Company)

1968 Mustang GT Convertible

In their second year of the new body design, Mustangs were still selling more than 300,000 units annually.

The options list for the 1968 Mustangs included AM/FM stereo radio, full-width front seat, speed control, SelectShift Cruise-O-Matic, eight-track Stereo-Sonic tape, four-speed manual transmission, tilt-away steering wheel and SelectAire conditioning. (Photo: Ford Motor Company)

A convertible was the perfect model for a
Mustang addict. The very nature of the buyer
said he or she was looking for some fun in life
at an affordable price. You could still buy a
six-cylinder convertible for $2,814, or for an
extra $105 you could have a V-8.

ONTARIO
SXTY ♣8
YOURS TO DISCOVER

1968 Mustang GT Convertible

1968 Mustang GT Convertible

Like the coupes, the convertibles changed little for 1968.

Mustang interiors kept the passengers low to the ground, with plenty of front seat legroom.

Short of the monster 428 Cobra Jet option, a buyer could have V-8 displacements of 289, 302 or 390 cubic inches.

As from the start, the gas filler was still located at the rear center.

The three vertical lights on either side were carried over from 1967.

With a full-size spare filling up the trunk, convertible owners could plan on carrying their golf clubs in the backseat!

1968 Shelby GT500KR

By the middle of the production year, Shelby changed all GT500 models to GT500KR, for King of the Road.

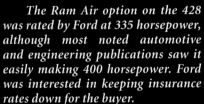

The Ram Air option on the 428 was rated by Ford at 335 horsepower, although most noted automotive and engineering publications saw it easily making 400 horsepower. Ford was interested in keeping insurance rates down for the buyer.

The unique Shelby front end and hood body pieces easily kept the car from being mistaken for a standard Mustang.

The large spoiler and Thunderbird sequential taillights told everyone this was a Cobra family member.

GT500s could be ordered with manual four-speed or automatic transmissions.

The Shelbys came with speed-rated Goodyear tires and styled wheels.

Functional side scoops added cooling for the rear brakes.

Shelby managed to provide a completely new look by adding a different hood and nose section to the production Mustang fenders. It gave a more shark-like appearance, befitting the big engine and rumbling exhausts.

Although rated at only 335 horsepower for insurance purposes, the King of the Road GT500 apparently produced closer to 400 horsepower according to several major magazine testing organizations.

Shelby Mustang

By 1968 the Shelby Mustang had continued to evolve, becoming more of a fast Thunderbird rather than a sports car. The 1967 Shelby sales were far greater than those of the 1966 models, and production was growing beyond what the Shelby American facilities could handle. The 1968 models would be built under the direction of both Ford and Shelby at the A. O. Smith Company located in Ionia, Michigan, a small town between Lansing and Grand Rapids. Rail cars shipped Shelby-bound Mustangs in "knock down" form

1968 Model Car Pricing

Falcon
4-door Sedan..........................$2,301
Futura 4-door Sedan.............$2,456
Futura Squire Wagon............$2,728

Fairlane
4-door Sedan I-6..................$2,464
4-door Sedan V-8..................$2,551

Fairlane 500
2-door Hardtop I-6................$2,568
2-door Hardtop V-8...............$2,679
Convertible V-8.....................$2,910

Fairlane Torino
4-door Sedan I-6...................$2,688
2-door Hardtop V-8...............$2,798
Squire Wagon V-8................$3,119
GT 2-door Fastback V-8.........$2,747
GT Convertible V-8................$3,001

Custom
4-door Sedan I-6...................$2,642
4-door Sedan V-8..................$2,749

Custom 500
4-door Sedan V-8..................$2,848

Galaxie 500
4-door Sedan V-8..................$2,971
2-door Fastback Coupe V-8.....$2,988
Convertible V-8.....................$3,215

Galaxie 500XL
2-door Fastback Coupe...........$3,092
Convertible V-8.....................$3,321

LTD
2-door Hardtop Coupe V-8......$3,153

Mustang
Coupe I-6.............................$2,602
Convertible I-6......................$2,814
Fastback I-6.........................$2,712

Station Wagons
Country Squire 9-passenger V-8........$3,619

Thunderbird
Hardtop 2-door.....................$4,716
Landau 2-door......................$4,845
Landau 4-door......................$4,924

mounted on the frame, fitting cleanly under the soft top.

All 1968 models used the Thunderbird sequential taillights, which blinked in sequence from center to the left or right, indicating the direction of the turn. The California and New Jersey cars received the same lights but were not allowed by state law to use the sequential system.

The 1968 GT500 came standard with the Ford Police Interceptor 428 engine, pumping out a healthy 360 hp at 5,400 rpm. By mid-1968, all Shelby GT500s had become GT500KR (King of the Road) models, powered by the 428 Cobra Jet Ram Air engine. Interestingly enough, Ford decided to rate the advertised horsepower on the low side, dropping it from the previous 360 hp to 335 hp. After numerous road tests and quarter mile runs, professional testing organizations agreed the actual output was much closer to 400 horsepower. Apparently Ford hoped to keep insurance affordable for the consumer and possibly sandbag the competition with the lower rating.

The GT500 started at $4,317 with few options, or for $4,438 you could have a convertible. (Photo: Ford Motor Company)

The Shelby GT500KR had unique front and rear design treatments to separate it clearly from the standard Mustang GT models.

from Ford's New Jersey plant to A. O. Smith for completion. By 1968 Ford had purchased the rights to the Cobra name and would be plastering it on non-Shelby-conceived vehicles during the coming years.

The new models were now available as convertibles in either the GT350 or GT500. They came with a built-in roll bar integrated into the body side panels and

The basic Mustang GT sold for $2,858 including a V-8 engine. The GT package also included a heavy-duty suspension and dual exhausts. (Photo: Ford Motor Company)

Ford was beginning to understand just how much their trucks added to the bottom line. In 1968 the F-100 light trucks alone contributed 285,000 units to Ford production, and the F-250 model added another 90,000 units.

1968 Ford F-100 Pickup

1968 Car Production

Fairlane
4-door	18,146
2-door Hardtop Formal	44,683

Fairlane 500
4-door	42,930
2-door Hardtop Formal	31,461
2-door Hardtop Bucket Seats	1,821
2-door Fastback	29,168
2-door Fastback Bucket Seats	3,284
Convertible	3,422
Convertible Bucket Seats	339

Fairlane GT
2-door Hardtop Formal	23,939
2-door Fastback	74,135
Convertible	5,310

Fairlane Torino
4-door Luxury	17,962
2-door Hardtop Formal	35,964

Fairlane Ranchero
Ranchero	5,014
Ranchero Standard	10,029
Ranchero GT	1,669

Fairlane Station Wagons
4-door Station Wagon	14,800
500 4-door Station Wagon	10,190
Torino Squire Wagon	14,773

Falcon
4-door	29,166
2-door	36,443

Falcon Futura
4-door	18,733
2-door	10,633
2-door Coupe Bucket Seats	10,077

Falcon Station Wagons
4-door Standard	15,576
4-door Futura	10,761

Ford Custom
4-door	45,980
2-door	18,485

Ford Custom 500
4-door	49,398
2-door	8,983

Galaxie 500
4-door	117,877
4-door Hardtop	55,461
2-door Hardtop	69,760
2-door Hardtop Formal	84,332
Convertible	11,832

Galaxie 500XL
2-door Hardtop	50,048
Convertible	6,066

Ford LTD
4-door	22,834
4-door Hardtop	61,755
2-door Hardtop Formal	54,163

Station Wagons
Country Sedan 6-passenger	39,335
Country Sedan 9-passenger	29,374
Ranch Wagon 6-passenger	18,237
Custom Ranch Wagon 6-pass.	18,181
Custom Ranch Wagon 9-pass.	13,421
Country Squire 6-passenger	33,994
Country Squire 9-passenger	57,776

Mustang
2-door Hardtop	233,472
2-door Hardtop Bench Seats	6,113
2-door Hardtop Deluxe	9,009
2-door Hardtop Deluxe Bench Seats	853
2-door Fastback	33,585
2-door Fastback Bench Seats	1,079
2-door Fastback Deluxe	7,661
2-door Fastback Deluxe Bench Seats	256
Convertible	22,037
Convertible Deluxe	3,339

Thunderbird
4-door Landau Bench Seats	17,251
4-door Landau Bucket Seats	4,674
2-door Hardtop Bench Seats	4,557
2-door Hardtop Bucket Seats	5,420
2-door Landau Bench Seats	13,924
2-door Landau Bucket Seats	19,105
Total	**1,770,055**

Ford Engines for 1968

CID	Carb.	Comp.	HP
Ford			
240 I-6	1 bbl	9.2	150 @ 4000
302 V-8	2 bbl	9.5	210 @ 4400
302 V-8	4 bbl	10.1	230 @ 4800
390 V-8	2 bbl	9.5	265 @ 4400
390 V-8	4 bbl	10.5	315 @ 4600
427 V-8	4 bbl	10.9	390 @ 5600
428 V-8	4 bbl	10.5	340 @ 4600
Fairlane/Torino			
200 I-6	1 bbl	9.2	115 @ 4400
302 V-8	2 bbl	9.5	210 @ 4400
390 V-8	2 bbl	9.5	265 @ 4400
390 V-8	4 bbl	10.5	325 @ 4800
427 V-8	4 bbl	10.9	390 @ 5600
428 V-8	4 bbl	10.6	335 @ 5400
Falcon			
170 I-6	1 bbl	9.1	100 @ 4400
200 I-6	1 bbl	9.2	115 @ 4400
289 V-8	2 bbl	9.3	195 @ 4400
302 V-8	4 bbl	10.1	230 @ 4800
Thunderbird			
390 V-8	4 bbl	10.5	315 @ 4600
429 V-8	4 bbl	10.5	360 @ 4600
Mustang			
200 I-6	1 bbl	9.2	115 @ 4400
289 V-8	2 bbl	9.3	195 @ 4400
302 V-8	4 bbl	10.1	230 @ 4800
390 V-8	2 bbl	10.5	280 @ 4400
390 V-8	4 bbl	10.5	325 @ 4800
427 V-8	4 bbl	10.9	390 @ 5600
428 V-8	4 bbl	10.6	335 @ 5400
Shelby Mustang			
302 V-8	4 bbl	10.5	250 @ 5000
428 V-8	4 bbl	10.6	335 @ 5200

In its second year of production, Bronco actually turned in lower sales figures than when it was introduced in 1966, making Ford wonder if this "SUV thing" would ever fly. (Photo: Ford Motor Company)

One writer at *Hot Rod* magazine said the GT500KR was "the fastest running pure-stock in the history of man."

The GT350 model came standard with a 302 Ford small-block V-8 producing a somewhat anemic 250 hp at 4,800 rpm with a Holley 600 four-barrel carburetor. You could also order the Paxton Supercharged engine and increase the power to 335 hp at 5,200 rpm.

The base GT350 pricing started at $4,116 and the convertible was $4,238. The GT500 was $4,317, or $4,438 for a convertible, and the KR model moved up to $4,472 for the Fastback or an additional $122 for the convertible.

▶

Mustang was still selling in huge numbers and, with new models like the Mach I, there didn't seem to be an end in sight. (Photo: Ford Motor Company)

FORD

The Year 1969

Ford Motor Company during the 1960s had been a major success story in products, profits and auto racing. It had captured racing wins at Le Mans, Daytona and Indianapolis. The company had also delivered outstanding new products with the Falcon, Fairlane, Mustang and Torino, and had kept the full-size Galaxie models selling at a record pace. Ford was also neck-and-neck with Chevrolet for truck leadership with its new I-Beam suspension F-Series.

Operations were in great shape in 1969, and global sales had increased by another 4 percent over 1968, including all Ford cars, trucks and tractors. The company's total worldwide sales hit a record U.S. $14.8 billion, up 122 percent over ten years, and it had invested $4.6 billion in worldwide facilities and

The Mustang Boss 429, known as the semi-Hemi, was built purposely to make the engine legal for NASCAR competition. Kar Kraft in Brighton, Michigan shoehorned the 429 V-8 into the tight engine bay for Ford.

equipment during the sixties. Ford North America (including Mexico and Canada) had increased sales by 72 percent since 1959. The company had increased U.S. sales by 50 percent during that same period. Ford North America produced 11 different car lines in 1969 compared to only five models in 1959.

Henry II warned Ford stockholders that while the company was in sound financial condition, labor and materials costs were rising and eating into profits. The U.S. government was also making an effort to slow the rate of inflation, which could cause a temporary slowdown in

auto sales as well. Henry II was also worried about the UAW union negotiations coming up in 1970, not knowing how they might affect future profits. He knew firsthand how a strike could devastate profits and sales leadership.

One of the more prophetic statements from Henry Ford II was about the four greatest challenges Ford would face during the seventies—the same ones that arose during the sixties. "The greatest challenge we will face in the seventies is the reduction of environmental pollution associated with the manufacture and use of motor vehicles." The other three challenges included equal opportunity for employment for all races, providing a better dealership experience to the customer and, last, improved automotive safety. Always an eloquent speaker, Henry II said to his stockholders, "It is clear that public opinion expects industry to contribute to the quality of life as never before. Your company's goal is to continue to prosper and grow by serving public expectations effectively and efficiently."

The Galaxie 500 two-door hardtop was the affordable, sporty Ford, at $3,070 including a V-8. (Photo: Ford Motor Company)

On September 11, 1969, Ford held a news conference to announce the dismissal of Bunkie Knudsen as president of Ford Motor Company. Lee Iacocca had never gotten along with Knudsen, seeing him as a ten-year setback to his drive to the top of Ford. After a combination of Ford politics and Knudsen's move to approve the 1972 model lineup without Henry II's input, Knudsen was let go. Iacocca was then made president of Ford North American Operations, one of three Ford presidents. Within a year he would make it to the top before misjudging the Ford leader's power and position—a mistake that would cost him his Ford job.

Even though the following decade would pose many challenges in environmental and automotive safety, Ford Motor Company would rise to the test. The company was a shining star at the end of the sixties, and Henry Ford II was not one to dodge a good contest, taking on all industry and government challenges.

Ford

To introduce the new models for 1969, Ford Division pulled together a hootenanny-style group of young people who would be featured in Ford television, radio, newspaper and magazine advertising. The group, dubbed The Going Thing, was founded specifically to use in advertising and, Ford hoped, add some excitement to the new car introductions. Ford also sponsored NFL Football, Wide World of Sports, Pro Bowlers Tour and spots on top variety shows in a heavy television advertising campaign.

The full-size Fords for 1969 came in Custom, Custom 500, Galaxie 500, XL, and LTD sedans, hardtops and convertibles. They were bigger in most respects, weighing in at 3,740 pounds, as

the hoods grew longer and the deck lids shorter in Mustang fashion. The base Custom models were given a simple chrome horizontal grille with fixed quad headlamps. The Galaxie 500, the mid-priced Ford, used the same fixed headlamps with a modified grille, while top-of-the-line LTD models had hidden headlamps and a full-width recessed grille protruding into a V-shape.

The Ford XL hardtop came with a new, sporty roofline Ford described as a "SportsRoof." The rear of the roof gave the impression of a fastback in profile, and the rear glass took on a much milder angle, leaving the C-pillars to extend almost to

the rear of the car on their own. Custom model two-door sedans came with a more traditional short, rounded roofline.

Ford introduced a new, energy-absorbing "S" frame chassis with curved front side

Ford sales literature referred to the 500XL hardtop as the SportsRoof.

The top-selling Ford wagon was the Country Squire model with stick-on "wood" and seating for 10. Ford moved 82,790 of these estate wagons in 1969.

The Galaxie 500 four-door was still Ford's big seller for the year, with 104,606 units rolling off the assembly line. (Photos this page: Ford Motor Company)

The base-model Ford Custom two-door sedan started at $2,632, a bargain for those wanting plenty of room, economy and a clean-looking body style.

You could be in the lap of luxury if you drove the Ford LTD convertible. It was available with a big 428 Cobra Jet V-8 if you really wanted to impress the neighbors. (Photos this page: Ford Motor Company)

speed manual, four-speed manual or Cruise-O-Matic, while the 360 hp 429 came with either a four-speed or Cruise-O-Matic only.

Overall performance, including power, steering responsiveness and handling, was improved over previous years as Ford tried to take the mush out of the LTD image. *Road Test* magazine in a 1969 article loved the vehicle, saying its entire staff gave it a score of 10 out of 10 points. "One of the very few cars which has produced any real excitement and surprise is the 1969 lush Ford—the LTD." The staff tested the 4,530-pound hardtop luxury sedan expecting a "soft, soggy slug of a car which would probably handle like a warm marshmallow—happily we were wrong on all points." They pointed out that the LTD, when fitted with the mass of options available, was certainly a luxury car and could hold its own with just about anything, including a Rolls-Royce.

Sitting on a 121-inch wheelbase (two inches longer than in 1968) the Ford provided an extra inch of rear legroom and two more inches of rear-seat shoulder space. The tread span was two inches wider, making it the widest in its class. Ford even advertised it as being "as wide as a Cadillac"!

Number one in the wagon market, Ford offered the Ranch Wagon, Custom 500 Ranch Wagon, Country Sedan, and the Galaxie 500 Country Squire. In 1966, Ford pioneered the two-way tailgate, opening as a tailgate or a door, and most of the competition followed a year or two later. The tailgate could now open as a door without lowering the window first. Fuel capacity had gone up from 20 to 23 gallons, extending miles between fill-ups, and a new, carpeted load floor option was now available. The carpet was held in place with snaps, permitting easy removal when hauling heavier cargo.

rails to provide a "crush zone" in the event of an accident. This was Ford's first effort at engineering safety into the structure of the vehicle. The new chassis also provided perimeter-type side rails to protect occupants from a side impact. Of course, their effectiveness was contingent upon another vehicle's bumper lining up with the side rail. A padded instrument panel, seatback locks for two-door models and energy absorbing armrests were carryover safety features.

Power trains for the new Fords started with the base 240 cubic inch I-6 or the optional 302 or 390 cubic inch V-8s with 220 and 265 horsepower. All three engines came with a three-speed manual transmission or a Cruise-O-Matic option. The Thunderjet 429 block was available in two different versions this year. The two-barrel model produced 320 hp and the four-barrel was rated at 360 hp, the same as for the Thunderbird. Both required premium fuel. The 320 hp model came with a three-

1969 Ford Options

220 hp 302 V-8	105.00
360 hp 429 V-8	237.07
4-speed manual transmission	194.31
Limited slip differential	41.60
Power front disc brakes	64.77
Bucket seats & console	168.62
Power windows	105.11
Automatic ride control system	89.94
SelectAire conditioner	388.74
Stereo-Sonic Tape System	133.86
GT Performance Group	259.09

Falcon

Described as "America's economy champ," Falcon was now nearing its end and had survived well, providing much-needed profits to Ford for a decade. After kicking off in 1960 with production figures approaching the half million mark, it rounded out 1969 with only 95,016 rolling off the assembly line.

After its glory years of performance Sprints and sporty looks, Falcon was now down to rather mundane looking base Falcon and Futura models. Both came in two- or four-door sedan and wagon styles or you could also choose Futura as a Sports Coupe.

Falcon engine choices were now the base 100 hp 170 cubic inch six or the optional derivative 200 cubic inch version producing 115 hp. Top-of-the-line power came from the optional 302 V-8 with 220 hp, available with a standard three-speed or optional four-speed manual or the SelectShift Cruise-O-Matic transmission.

Falcon boasted more interior room than any of the other Big Three compacts, and options included power front disc brakes, power steering, SelectAire conditioner, power tailgate window or two-way Magic Doorgate on wagons and a vinyl roof on two-door models. The Falcon wagon base price was $2,643.

The body was of a unitized construction for greater rigidity

The Falcon was in its last model year, although some minor production runs continued to 1970. It had served the Ford family well for a decade and had provided profits and solid, inexpensive transportation for many families. This would be the end of the road for the compact. (Photo: Ford Motor Company)

and was treated against corrosion and rust. This also helped with the "quietness quotient," keeping rattles and squeaks to a minimum. Extra insulation also kept it quieter and better insulated the passengers from the outside elements in winter or summer. The base two-door sedan weighed in at 2,818 pounds and the wagon, the heaviest, at 3,252 pounds.

With Maverick already introduced, Falcon was on its way out. Production of the Falcon continued into early 1970, when it changed over to the Torino base body for a 1970½ model. Falcon had been a great success, adding greatly to Ford Motor Company profits, but had simply run its course with other models now taking over. It continued to be produced in a similar form for many more years in Argentina and shipped to both Brazil and Venezuela. In Australia, where the nameplate is still in production, it evolved from the basic Falcon known to North Americans to a more Taurus-like sedan.

1969 Falcon Options

SelectShift transmission (w/V-8)	189.66
Power front disc brakes	64.77
Two-way Magic Doorgate (wagons)	45.39
Power steering	89.73
SelectAire conditioning	368.09
Wheel covers	21.34
Vinyl roof	79.09
Remote outside mirror	12.95
Full tinted windows	32.44

Fairlane/Torino

The model lineup for Ford's mid-size entries for 1969 was the Fairlane, Fairlane 500, Torino, Torino GT and Cobra. Ford, now owner of the Cobra name, was starting to label everything from car models to engines with the once-magic nameplate.

The Fairlane models came with a standard bright aluminum grille, the Torino and GT with a gray plastic grille with bright aluminum trim and the Cobra with a black painted aluminum grille. Torino or Fairlane 500

The Fairlane Cobra came standard with a 428 Cobra Jet V-8 producing 335 hp and 440 ft.-lbs. of torque. Four-on-the-floor was standard in the Cobra model, as were a healthy sounding set of dual exhausts and a heavy-duty suspension.

models could be ordered in either the formal hardtop or the SportsRoof Fastback, while the base Fairlanes came as two- or four-door sedans or hardtops only.

The Cobra model, also available as either a formal hardtop or SportsRoof, came with a three-dimensional chrome emblem to denote its performance status. If you ordered the Ram Air option, a hood scoop was added. A Super Cobra Jet, or SCJ, model was also available when you ordered the Ford Drag Pak that included either a 3.91 or 4.30 rear axle. It also had a standard engine oil cooler and no air conditioning was available.

Car Life magazine ran an in-depth performance test on the Torino Cobra 428 with Ram Air induction and invited a Ford public relations guy to come along. They surprised the Ford guest by including a modified Plymouth Road Runner in the test—but letting him think the Plymouth was stock. They figured it would be a great joke, watching his face as the Road Runner knocked the doors off the stock Cobra 428. "The joke was on us," declared the writer. "No, the Ford wasn't faster, but the Cobra pulled a hole shot on the Road Runner most runs, and never lost by more than two lengths." The writer expected to show readers how much more they could get for their money by hopping up a Road Runner, "but we learned that the big, plush Cobra can hold its own, even in a rigged match race."

The magazine road test did bring to light the Cobra's poor handling characteristics. There was plenty of understeer in the corners and oversteer could be induced at any time with the excess horsepower. The test revealed excellent brakes— optional power-assisted discs in front and drum in the rear.

Zero-to-60 mph was achieved in 7.3 seconds, and top speed was 125 at 6,000 rpm. Normal driving conditions recorded fuel consumption of 10.2 to 11.2 mpg. *Car Life* wrapped up the article by saying, "The Cobra's performance was surprisingly good, the price is within reason, [and] the fastback roof is the best looking around."

Another interesting model came out of Ford's need to succeed at NASCAR's super speedways. Finding the front of the Torino a little boxy for speeds of 200 mph, Ford decided to build the prerequisite number of 500 new models called the Torino Talladega to meet NASCAR's homologation standards. The Talladega used the standard Torino SportsRoof body with a six-inch longer curved nose and Cobra grille to make it competitive with the Dodge Chargers and even its sister Mercury Cyclone. A total of 754

While the base Fairlane two-door hardtop still accounted for the bulk of sales at 85,630 units, the Torino models accounted for almost a third of the total Fairlane production.

For $3,073 you could ride in style with a new 1969 Fairlane Torino GT convertible. (Photos this page: Ford Motor Company)

Talladega models were built, all in the Atlanta assembly plant. The front bumper of the Talladega was nothing more than a rear bumper cut and rewelded to fit under the new grille. It was used because it was smaller than the original front bumper and nicely sloped better to cut down on wind resistance.

Available in Wimbledon White, Royal Maroon or Presidential Blue, the Talladega standard performance features included a 335 hp, four-barrel 428 Cobra Jet engine, oil cooler, cast aluminum rocker covers, extra-cooling package, 55-ampere alternator, 80-ampere hour battery, SelectShift Cruise-O-Matic transmission and power front disc brakes. All Talladegas came with a non-gloss black hood and F70 x 14 Firestone Wide-Oval tires. Ram Air was optional on the Talladega.

The wind tunnel testing was highly successful for Ford. Richard Petty abandoned the Plymouth camp to win his first time out in the Talladega at the Riverside 500. This was followed by Lee Roy Yarbrough's win at the Daytona 500 in February. Ford won 26 of the 54 races that year, and the driver's championship went to David Pearson in his Talladega. Dodge Charger was left with 22 wins, Plymouth with two and Mercury with four. The early events were run with the older 427-wedge engine until homologation was met for the 429 semi-Hemi.

Fairlane engines for 1969 included the standard 250 cubic inch, 155 hp inline six engine, the 220 hp 302 V-8, the 250 or 290 hp 351 V-8s. The top-of-the-line power came with the big 428 Cobra Jet rated at 335 hp with or without the Ram Air option. The 428 V-8s came standard with four-wheel drum brakes or optional front power disc brakes and four-speed manual or SelectShift Cruise-O-Matic transmissions.

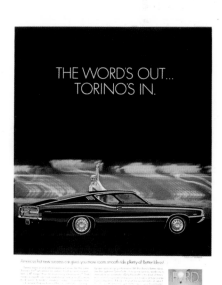

THE WORD'S OUT...
TORINO'S IN.

Referring to the top-of-the-line Fairlane as a Torino gave buyers the impression that it was a totally new model line when in fact it was still a Fairlane.

1969 Talladega

Ford desperately needed a car that could cut through the air at 200 mph at super speedways like Daytona and Talladega. Out of Ford's Atlanta assembly plant came the new Torino Talladega with a longer, sloped nose, a smaller front bumper (made out of a rear bumper) and a new Boss 429 power plant. Only 754 Talladegas were built, enough to cover the 500 production cars required by NASCAR to be considered legal for racing. In the first race at Daytona, the Talladega had to run with the 427-wedge engine but still won the event.

Wagons came in Fairlane, Fairlane 500 or Torino Squire models. All came standard with the Ford two-way Magic Doorgate and an optional rear-facing third seat. The second seat would easily fold down with a push-button release for more cargo capacity. Total production for Fairlane/ Torino this year was a healthy 386,366 vehicles.

1969 Torino/Fairlane/Cobra Options

320 hp 390 V-8	287.53
335 hp 428 V-8 Cobra Jet Ram Air	133.44
4-speed manual transmission	194.31
Power front disc brakes	64.77
Power windows	105.11
Power full-width seat	100.15
Rim Blow Deluxe steering wheel	35.70
Intermittent windshield wipers	16.85
Vinyl roof	90.15
Competition suspension	30.64
Limited slip differential	41.60

Thunderbird

Now in its third year of the same body style and getting larger and more luxurious by the year, Thunderbird had steadily dropped

Thunderbird had gone into the luxury market, hoping that a touch of sportiness would still linger from the days of old. The T-Bird now came with a heated rear glass area for quick defrosting, and the sunroof was still a popular option.

in volume from almost 80,000 in 1967 to around 49,000 in 1969.

In a 1969 *Motor Trend* road test, the Landau hardtop averaged a respectable 16.8 mpg on one stretch of highway with the massive 429 four-barrel V-8. One improvement for the new Thunderbirds was a fail-safe system for the retractable headlamps. If the vacuum system failed, the headlamps would automatically flip to the open position until you could make it to the dealer for repairs. Cornering lights for lighting up the left or right side of the road when turning were now standard on all models.

The now-famous wall-to-wall taillights were dropped in 1969, "because they had been copied so much" according to Ford. The Thunderbird went back to wide, separated taillights and kept the sequential directional feature. Backup lights were hidden behind the chrome grille between the taillights. The best-selling Thunderbird was the Landau hardtop with the new formal vinyl roof, leaving rear-seat passengers with no rear window. The Landau models offered an optional power sliding sunroof with a manual crank in case the motor should fail. Another first was a heated backlight glass option that zapped frost in minutes.

The Landau hardtop weighed in at 4,549 pounds and the four-door model exactly 100 pounds more. The standard and only engine was the 429 cubic inch V-8 producing 360 hp and 460 ft.-lbs. of torque.

1969 Thunderbird Options

Electric sunroof	453.30
Power antenna	28.97
6-way power seat	98.89
Power windows	109.22
Rear defogger	22.33
Speed control	97.21
Tilt-away steering wheel	66.14
AM/FM stereo radio	150.29
Four-note horn	15.59

Mustang

Mustangs were offered in several interesting configurations in 1969 for a couple of reasons. First, Ford needed to make certain it had the right car for all the right "sporty car" buyers. This would range from the Grandé luxury buyer to the Mach I power buyer. The second consideration in bringing out new models was to qualify, or "homologate," cars and engines for both the Trans Am series and NASCAR stock car racing. The Boss 302 Mustang was the candidate for Trans Am and Ford had to produce at least 1,000 units to qualify. In NASCAR, the rules stated that for a new engine to qualify for its events, 500 had to be built but could be sold in any car. The engine just had to be on the streets in a registered car. So Ford chose to drop the newly developed 429 semi-Hemi into a Mustang even though it would be campaigned in a Torino Talladega at the tracks.

The purpose-built Boss 429, based on the new SportsRoof body was actually built for Ford at Kar Kraft in Brighton, Michigan. Kar Kraft had also built the Ford GT Mark IV that won the 1967 Le Mans 24-Hour. Shoehorning the big 429 block into the engine bay was Kar Kraft's biggest challenge. They had to move the shock towers outward by an inch on either side to make more room and modify the front suspension accordingly. This gave the Boss 429 a wider stance than its cousins. Interestingly enough, the acceleration times were not all that impressive in street form. Zero-to-60 mph took 7.1 seconds and the quarter mile was just over 14 seconds at 102 mph. The sole purpose of the big Boss cars was to get the engine in NASCAR—not make it a top street performer. Only 857 Boss 429 Mustangs were built, but that was all Ford really needed. It was never intended to have a large production run.

1969 Mustang Boss 429

Though an impressive performer, the Boss 429 was not as fast as the Boss 302 in factory trim. Its sole purpose in life was to put more than 500 of the 429 engines on the road to qualify it for NASCAR competition. It didn't matter to NASCAR that the Boss 429 engine was in a Mustang on the street and in a Torino Talladega on the track.

Introduced in April 1969, the small-block Boss 302 quickly became a street legend and was given rave reviews by most of the key auto journalists. The magazines typically chose the Boss 302 over either the Mach I or the famed Boss 429 because of its overall performance and handling characteristics. It was an efficient performance car and well balanced. Unlike the Boss 429, the Boss 302 was initially planned to be a volume production vehicle in answer to Chevrolet's Z-28. Producing 290 hp, the modified 302 V-8 came with a Holley 680 cfm carburetor, aluminum high-rise intake manifold and mechanical lifters. Actual horsepower was considered somewhat greater than what Ford was advertising. Nailing down a zero-to-60 mph time of 6.9 seconds and a quarter mile time of 14.98 seconds at 96 mph, it could dust off a Torino

Cobra Jet 428. The Boss 302 came only in Wimbledon White, Calypso Coral, Bright Yellow and Acapulco Blue. Between April and September 1, 628 Boss 302 models were produced and sold, easily meeting SCCA's Trans Am homologation rules.

Mustangs in general stayed with the 108-inch wheelbase and grew in both dimensions and in weight. The new Mustangs were now more than 150 pounds heavier on average and four inches longer than the 1968 models. They were also a half-inch lower. It wasn't that the total body size grew so much as that the front nose was stretched out longer and now accommodated quad headlamps, two of which were mounted in the grille. The body side was now smooth without the scooped-out panels of before. There was a small, non-functional air vent mounted just in front of the rear wheels on the base

models, convertible and Grandé, but not on the Mach I, Boss 302 or SportsRoof models. SportsRoof models came with a non-functioning air scoop located just below the rear swing-out windows.

Interiors were larger, adding two and a half inches of legroom in the rear seat, more shoulder and hip room up front and a foot-operated parking brake in place of the pull-up handle between the seats. Vent windows were also deleted, and now all Mustangs came with adjustable cowl vents to let in plenty of fresh air.

In a March 1969 Motor Trend article comparing the Mustang Mach I with the Javelin, Cougar, Camaro and Firebird, the writer commented, "The Ford boys have done it again." The test found the Mach I put the competition away in just about all categories. "Don't mess with the ponies. That's right, man. Mach I puts Mustang back where it all started—Numero Uno."

Standard in the $3,139 Mach I was the 351 V-8 with a two-barrel carburetor, producing 250 hp. For an extra $25.91 over the Mach I base price, you could have a four-barrel 290 horsepower 351—not a bad investment at 62 cents per horsepower.

The Mustang Grandé was mostly a dress-up package with a softer suspension than the other models. The package included sound insulation, molded door panels, "luxury" cloth and vinyl seat trim, "woodlike" three-spoke steering wheel and dash trim, and an electric clock. *Car Life* magazine tested the Grandé on a rainy day and gave it a top rating for nimbleness. "The Grandé sliced through the wet, wheeling happily around the handling

circuit going where the driver wanted, quickly and quietly. When the designers put the comfort in, they didn't take Mustang's traditional nimbleness out."

The Mustang equipped with the 351 V-8 was a well-balanced vehicle with a reputation for getting through the curves quickly. Performance from the 290 hp, four-barrel 351 V-8 was a little less than you might expect, managing a zero-to-60 mph time of only seconds and a quarter mile time of 15.59 seconds at 89 mph. The Mach I also offered this engine as an option. Fuel consumption under normal conditions ranged from 12 to 15 mpg.

Engines for Mustang in 1969 started with the 115 hp 200 I-6 or the optional 250 cubic inch, 155 hp six. Also available were the 220 hp 302 V-8, 250 or 290 hp 351 V-8, 320 hp 390 V-8 or 335 hp 428 V-8, also available with Ram Air. The 428 engines came with a standard extra cooling package, an 80-ampere hour battery and a functioning hood scoop. The 290 horsepower 302 was available by April 1969 only in the Boss 302 model.

Iacocca and asked him to cancel the program. I thought there were lots of other cars built by other companies that were similar, and the competition was much keener, including inside Ford Motor Company. I saw insurance rates going up. And I could see the government putting a stop to horsepower advertising and speed, and more and more bureaucratic regulations coming up every day."

With Ford producing the Shelby Mustangs alongside competing Boss 302 and 429 models and the new Mach I, there really was no room for the ever-heavier, more luxurious Shelby models.

By September Shelby Mustang production was ended after sales slowed dramatically. The amazing vehicles had experienced a great production run but now the window of opportunity had closed.

Maverick

Was it possible Ford was getting superstitious? Before the demise of the Falcon, the company had the new Maverick ready to go. Just to make sure it was a success, they borrowed engines and other parts from the Falcon, Fairlane and Mustang and had decided to introduce it in April 1969, exactly five years after the Mustang. It came with a $1,995 price tag, per Iacocca's instructions, and weighed in at 2,487 pounds. Iacocca's original goal was $1,995 at 1,995 pounds, but the weight target could not realistically be met.

These 1969½ Mavericks, identified as a 1970 model by Ford, came only in a two-door sedan and had few options. Air conditioning was available for $380 and an automatic transmission for $201. There was also an appearance group option that included carpets, stainless window trim, a radio and 14-inch wheels.

Ford Engines for 1969

CID	Carb.	Comp.	HP
Ford			
240 I-6	1 bbl	9.2	150 @ 4000
302 V-8	2 bbl	9.5	220 @ 4400
390 V-8	2 bbl	9.5	265 @ 4400
429 V-8	2 bbl	10.9	320 @ 5600
429 V-8	4 bbl	10.5	360 @ 4600
Fairlane/Torino			
250 I-6	1 bbl	9.2	155 @ 4400
302 V-8	2 bbl	9.5	220 @ 4400
351 V-8	2 bbl	9.5	250 @ 4600
351 V-8	4 bbl	10.7	290 @ 4800
390 V-8	4 bbl	10.5	320 @ 4800
428 V-8	4 bbl	10.6	335 @ 5200
Falcon			
170 I-6	1 bbl	9.1	100 @ 4400
200 I-6	1 bbl	9.2	115 @ 4400
302 V-8	2 bbl	9.5	220 @ 4800
Thunderbird			
429 V-8	4 bbl	10.5	360 @ 4600
Mustang			
200 I-6	1 bbl	9.2	115 @ 4400
250 I-6	1 bbl	9.2	155 @ 4400
302 V-8	2 bbl	9.5	220 @ 4800
302 V-8	4 bbl	10.5	290 @ 5800
351 V-8	2 bbl	9.5	250 @ 4600
351 V-8	4 bbl	10.7	290 @ 4800
390 V-8	4 bbl	10.5	320 @ 4800
428 V-8	4 bbl	10.5	335 @ 4600
429 V-8	4 bbl	10.5	360 @ 4600
Shelby Mustang			
351 V-8	4 bbl	10.7	290 @ 4800
428 V-8	4 bbl	10.6	335 @ 5200

1969 Mustang Options

290 hp 351 V-8	84.25
320 hp 390 V-8	158.08
335 hp 428 V-8 Ram Air Cobra Jet	420.96
4-speed manual transmission	204.64
Traction-Lok differential	63.51
High-back bucket seats	84.25
Electric clock	15.59
Competition suspension	30.64
SelectAire conditioner	379.57
Stereo-Sonic Tape	133.84
Console	53.82
Full tinted windows	32.44
Dual racing mirrors	19.48

Shelby Mustang

In an article by Roy Ames, Carroll Shelby described the death of his Mustang in 1969. "I went to Mr.

1969 Mustang Mach 1

The Mustang Mach I came with a two-barrel carburetor 351 V-8 and performance suspension. The sloping roofline was called the SportsRoof, according to Ford literature.

1969 Mustang Boss 429

Ford GT Mark IV builder Kar Kraft
produced 857 Boss 429 Mustangs for Ford.

1969 Mustang Boss 429

The 1969 Boss 429 Mustangs were available in five colors: Wimbledon White, Royal Maroon, Raven Black, Black Jade and Candy Apple Red.

Kar Kraft had to move the shock towers outward by an inch on either side and modify the suspension to accommodate the big-block semi-Hemi.

All Boss 429s came with chrome 15x7 Magnum 500 wheels and F60x15 Goodyear Polyglas GT tires.

The Boss 429 front end sits lower than those of the Boss 302 or Mach I Mustangs.

1969 Shelby GT500

Shelby convertibles all came with a standard roll bar, in the expectation their owners would have a heavy foot.

Backseat space was tight and the roll bar made head bumping a regular event.

By 1969 the Shelby Mustangs had gotten heavier and become just another hot Mustang. This would be the last year for the Shelby Mustang. Ford's Mach I, Boss 429 and Boss 302 models were all similar, and customers were no longer willing to pay a premium price for the Shelbys.

GT500 convertibles sold for $5,027.

Early Mavericks came with a 144 cubic inch six as the base engine, but it was completely underpowered and Ford soon made the Falcon workhorse 170 cubic inch I-6 standard. It came with reworked intake and exhaust manifold improvements and four main bearings, producing 100 hp at 4,400 rpm. The optional 200 cubic inch version of the base engine produced 115 horsepower.

Maverick was off to a healthy start. Between its April introduction and the September new model year, Ford produced 127,833 of the new two-door sedans. And with Ford considering all Mavericks as 1970 models, it had a first model year run of 18 months in which it sold more than 579,000 units.

End of an Era

The close of the decade of the sixties, one of performance and style, would find the automotive industry left with a new decade of underperforming, bland vehicles. Meeting new government emissions controls and Corporate Average Fuel Economy (CAFE) mandates would soak up auto

The Mach I, 351 Windsor V-8 had plenty of horsepower and torque, especially in the optional 290 hp four-barrel version.

A Cobra Jet 335 horsepower 428 engine was also available in the Mach I Mustang, but the extra weight made it a less capably handling machine compared to the Boss 302 model.

1969 Model Car Pricing

Falcon

4-door Sedan I-6	$2,316
Wagon I-6	$2,643
Futura 2-door Sports Coupe V-8	$2,671
Futura Station Wagon V-8	$2,844

Fairlane

4-door Sedan I-6	$2,471
4-door Sedan V-8	$2,561

Fairlane 500

4-door Sedan V-8	$2,641
2-door Fastback Coupe V-8	$2,674
Convertible V-8	$2,924

Fairlane Torino

4-door Sedan V-8	$2,806
GT 2-door Fastback Coupe	$2,823
GT Convertible	$3,073
Cobra Fastback Coupe	$3,183
Cobra Hardtop Coupe	$3,208

Custom

4-door Sedan I-6	$2,674
4-door Sedan V-8	$2,779

Custom 500

4-door Sedan V-8	$2,878
2-door Sedan V-8	$2,632

Galaxie 500

2-door Fastback Coupe V-8	$3,070

Galaxie 500XL

2-door Fastback Coupe	$3,157
Convertible V-8	$3,385

LTD

4-door Sedan V-8	$3,192
Country Squire 10-passenger V-8	$3,721

Mustang

Coupe I-6	$2,635
Convertible I-6	$2,849
Mach I V-8	$3,139
Boss 302	$3,588
Boss 429	$4,798

Thunderbird

Coupe	$4,807
Landau 2-door Hardtop	$4,947
Landau 4-door Hardtop	$5,026

manufacturers' resources and energy. Manufacturers also had to divert massive sums of money, time and energy to meeting new safety regulations demanding new cars that were more "crushable." Fortunately, Ford had already moved ahead in this arena, making the front portions of their cars, instead of the passenger compartment, absorb the energy of an impact. More effective seat belts that were easier to use would also be high on the safety-improvement list.

Although the bland automotive period of the 1970s would ultimately clean up much of our air and make our vehicles safer to drive, it put all performance and style on hold for almost 15 years. The sixties would be the last decade of high-horsepower street machines with NASCAR-style engines for many years. For Ford Motor Company the sixties was about much more than just horsepower, although there was plenty of it in the Ford stables. The decade was about a company that was financially viable under Henry Ford II's leadership, a company that showed its pride in many forms. When Ferrari wouldn't sell to Ford, Henry II put the big blue machine in gear, winning four straight Le Mans events while dominating most of NASCAR, drag racing and road racing during the same period. He Okayed Iacocca's Mustang idea, opening the way for a completely new segment in the market while making huge profits for Ford.

Ford Motor Company contracted charismatic leaders like Lee Iacocca and Bunkie Knudsen, led by Henry II. These brilliant automotive strategists and real "car guys" knew what the public wanted and what would make profits. The Ford Design Department had Gene Bordinat to lead the team and designers like Joe Oros to give them the Mustang —a design finished in only two weeks.

The Super Spoiler was based on a Mercury design but was never seriously considered as a production model. (Photo: Ford Motor Company)

Maybe your second car should be more than just another first car

These better-idea Fords can do things your first car can't

FORD

Ford advertised its F-Series, Ranchero, Bronco and Econoline models as second vehicles that could do things your first car could not. The group was described as a sporty group of utility vehicles.

Ford Motor Company produced 343,746 of the popular F-100 series 2WD and 4WD pickups in 1969. The interiors were becoming more luxurious as buyers added more options and could use their trucks to go to church on Sunday.

1969 Ford F-100 Pickup

1969 Car Production

Fairlane
- 4-door 27,296
- 2-door Hardtop Formal 85,630

Fairlane 500
- 4-door 40,888
- 2-door Hardtop Fastback 22,504
- 2-door Hardtop Fastback
  - Bucket Seats 7,345
- 2-door Hardtop Formal 24,800
- 2-door Hardtop Formal
  - Bucket Seats 3,379
- Convertible 2,045
- Convertible Bucket Seats 219

Fairlane Ranchero
- Ranchero 5,856
- Ranchero 500 11,214
- Ranchero GT 1,658
- Ranchero GT Bucket Seats 727

Fairlane Station Wagons
- Fairlane 10,882
- Fairlane 500 Wagon 12,869

Fairlane Torino
- 4-door 11,971
- 2-door Hardtop Formal 20,789
- Torino Squire Wagon 14,472

Torino GT
- 2-door Hardtop Fastback
  - Bucket Seats 20,440
- 2-door Hardtop Fastback
  - Bench Seats 40,879
- 2-door Hardtop Formal
  - Bench Seats 12,883
- Convertible Bucket Seats 928

- Convertible Bench Seats 1,624
- 2-door Hardtop Formal
  - Bucket Seats 5,068

Falcon
- 4-door 22,719
- 2-door 29,263

Falcon Futura
- 4-door 11,850
- 2-door 6,482
- Sports Coupe Bucket Seats 5,931

Falcon Wagons
- Falcon 11,568
- Futura 7,203

Ford Custom
- 4-door 45,653

Ford Custom 500
- 4-door 45,761
- 2-door 15,439

Galaxie 500
- 4-door 104,606
- 4-door Hardtop 64,031
- 2-door 7,585
- 2-door Hardtop Formal 71,920
- 2-door Hardtop Fastback 63,921
- Convertible 6,910

Ford LTD
- 4-door 63,709
- 4-door Hardtop 113,168
- 2-door Hardtop Formal 111,565

Ford Wagons
- Custom 500, 6-passenger 16,432
- Country Squire 6-passenger 46,445

- Country Squire 10-passenger 82,790
- Country Sedan 6-passenger 36,287
- Country Sedan 10-passenger 27,517
- Ranch Wagon 6-passenger 17,489
- Ranch Wagon 10-passenger 11,563

Ford XL
- 2-door Hardtop Fastback 54,557
- Convertible 7,402

Maverick
- 2-door Sedan 127,833

Mustang
- 2-door Fastback 56,022
- 2-door Fastback Deluxe 5,958

Mustang Mach I
- 2-door Hardtop 118,613
- 2-door Hardtop Bench Seats 4,131
- 2-door Hardtop Deluxe 5,210
- 2-door Hardtop Deluxe Bench Seats ... 504
- 2-door Hardtop Grandé 22,182
- 2-door Fastback 72,458
- Convertible 11,307
- Convertible Deluxe 3,439

Thunderbird
- 4-door Landau Bucket Seats 1,983
- 4-door Landau Bench Seats 13,712
- 2-door Hardtop Bucket Seats 2,361
- 2-door Hardtop Bench Seats 3,552
- 2-door Landau Hardtop
  - Bucket Seats 12,425
- 2-door Landau Hardtop
  - Bench Seats 15,239

Total — **1,973,061**

In racing, Plymouth's Hemi became a problem for the Torino. Henry II's engineers went to work and came up with a 429 semi-Hemi while the designers were in the wind tunnel putting together the Torino Talladega—problem solved. For Henry II teamwork was everything. He didn't mind fully funding projects, and he expected nothing less than complete success in return.

For Henry II business wasn't about only steel and money. He cared deeply about his employees and strove to make society a better place. Henry II stressed the need to hire people from all walks of life, knowing that this would help society and the communities where Ford was doing business. He always believed in giving something back to the communities where Ford

owned facilities, making those towns and cities better places for people to live.

One of the most important aspects of Ford Motor Company's success has been the continual involvement of the family since its beginning in 1903. Henry II took over Ford from his grandfather, Henry Ford, in 1945 and kept his hand on the wheel for 35 years, as first president then chairman of the Dearborn-based company. Even Henry II's son, Edsel, and nephew, Bill Ford Jr., served on the board of directors. Bill Ford Jr. is now the chairman of the company, bringing it completely under the family's watchful eye once again.

Ford Motor Company's decades-long string of successes in vehicles, sales, racing,

engineering and design speaks for itself. "If you look at our 100-year history," said chairman Bill Ford Jr., "it is clear that our success always has been driven by our products and our people. Great products made us what we are, and they will take us where we're going in the future." It's been more than a hundred years since Henry set up business, and the products just keep on coming. Ford's future looks great.

▶

Driven by Americans Ronnie Bucknum and Dick Hutcherson, this #5 GT40 MK II was powered by a NASCAR-style 427-wedge engine. They placed third in the 1966 Ford sweep of Le Mans. (Photo: Ford Motor Company)

FORD

Ford Racing

During the 1960s, there were many great Ford racing victories and most have been well documented in hundreds of books and magazines. This chapter is not meant to be a chapter of statistics or a blow-by-blow account of each event. It is rather a collection of personal stories that paint the scene of craziness, speed and personalities with behind-the-scenes anecdotes of one of Ford racing's most interesting eras.

Ford was officially absent from racing from 1957 to 1962. The Automobile Manufacturers Association (AMA), an organization made up largely of the heads of major auto manufacturers, had set a racing ban in place after several years of grisly deaths of both drivers and spectators. There was also increasing political pressure from Congress. Finally the heads of the AMA agreed on June 6, 1957, that auto manufacturers would no longer have any association with or support auto racing of any sort.

The customer is king, however, and it didn't take manufacturers long to realize that the American public enjoyed horsepower and auto racing. Deciding to listen more closely to the people holding the money, Ford started supporting racing teams by providing engines, technical assistance and money to help them stay ahead of the competition. By 1962 Ford Motor

In this 1-2-3 sweep of the 1966 24 hours of Le Mans, Carroll Shelby, Leo Beebe and Henry II ordered the cars to cross the line together to provide the now famous finish line photo. Unfortunately, Le Mans officials noted that since the #2 car had started approximately 30 yards in back of the Miles/Hulme #1 car, it had traveled farther and therefore was the winner even though it actually crossed the line a few feet behind the #1 car. The #1 car had been leading and would have won, only it slowed under orders for the photo finish. (Photo: Ford Motor Company)

Company had endured the ban long enough, and Henry Ford II wrote a letter to the AMA saying that Ford would "no longer honor the 1957 agreement and would police its involvement with auto racing internally." Thank you very much.

Ford had already been supporting their stock car teams through Holman-Moody, a well-organized North Carolina racing operation that had been building and driving stock cars for years. Owners John Holman and Ralph Moody had kept Ford in the forefront of NASCAR events during the supposed ban.

Fearless Freddy

In 1960 Fred Lorenzen was a talented and struggling young carpenter/stock car racer following the Midwest racing circuits. The Chicago native owned and drove his own car and was spotted racing at a Wisconsin dirt track by Ralph Moody.

Moody quickly signed him to drive for Holman-Moody on the 1961 NASCAR circuit, and his success helped Ford to sell sedans for the next few years.

At the 1961 Darlington Rebel 300 convertible race Lorenzen was pitted against Curtis Turner, also in a Ford. Moody knew Turner well and he said, "Freddy, this guy is crafty and good. He'll do anything to win. You watch him or he'll put you right out of the racetrack just to pass you. He's just mean as hell. Just be careful."

"He knew that we were the two fastest cars out there," said Lorenzen. Both drivers started on the front row together and fought back and forth most of the day. With about 40 laps to go Lorenzen blew a tire, sending him in to the wall and bending a fender. But the crew got him back on the track almost a lap down from Turner. Driving at a torrid pace, Lorenzen was gaining more than a second a lap. The crowd was on its feet cheering with only seven laps to go as Lorenzen closed the gap. As he flashed by the front pit lane Moody held up a pit sign saying, "Use your head."

"With two laps to go I was on the outside coming off of [turn] four and I built the momentum up. When I went to pass him, he put me into the wall, chunks of concrete went flying, and it pushed the whole side of my car in," but not enough to make Lorenzen pit. With Turner still in the lead and going into turn one, Moody held up a sign that said, "Think."

"So down the backstretch I backed out of it to go into turn three and I built the momentum way up going into turn four. So I'm coming up on him maybe five or six miles an hour as we come off of four and I faked him to the outside and he moved up on the wall. Then I jumped under him on the inside on the white flag and I took the lead." On the backstretch Turner had his front bumper touching Lorenzen, pushing him all the way. They rounded turn four with Lorenzen still in the lead and the crowd went crazy as he took the checkered flag. Then going into turn one Turner moved in and hit Lorenzen's car in the rear, but the former Illinois carpenter already had the win in his pocket. "That was the biggest racing moment of my life."

Lorenzen had his heroes from his Chicago childhood. "Oh, yes, that's why I went into racing. When I was 12 and I used to lay in the backyard in my tent and I always listened to the Southern 500. The big men were always Fireball Roberts, Joe Weatherly, Curtis Turner and Junior Johnson. My hero was Fireball."

In 1963 Lorenzen inherited Fireball Roberts as his teammate at Holman-Moody, and they had a good year together. In the 1964 season the dynamic pair of drivers had been busy, with Lorenzen capturing five wins going into the Charlotte World 600 event. Roberts had only one win for the year and

Racing Timeline

- 1960—Ford begins its Total Performance program of the 1960s, working to develop competitive vehicles in Indy, NASCAR and Le Mans racing circles.
- 1961—Ford signs "Fearless Freddy" Lorenzen to drive for Holman-Moody, and wins at Martinsville, Darlington and Atlanta to save a difficult year in NASCAR.
- 1962—Seeing few stock car wins, Ford works to develop the 427 V-8 and sleek body styles for the next season. Lorenzen and Nelson Stacy salvage the season with a half dozen wins.
- 1962—Lorenzen, Ralph Moody and Don White set 46 national and international speed records at the Bonneville Salt Flats in Freddy's #28 Ford.
- 1963—Ford wins its first Daytona 500, taking the first five positions. Fireball Roberts takes the July Daytona event in his Ford Galaxie Fastback. Ford continues its march to the top, winning 23 of 55 events.
- 1963—Dave MacDonald and Ken Miles drive Shelby Cobras to first and second place at Riverside, beating the new Corvette Stingrays.
- 1964—Ford introduces its double overhead cam V8 Indy car engine. Jim

- Clark wins Indianapolis 500 pole in a Lotus-Ford. Fred Lorenzen wins 8 of 16 events entered, driving a Holman-Moody Ford.
- 1964—Cobra Daytona Coupe wins GT Class at Le Mans (fourth overall).
- 1965—Jim Clark scores Ford's first victory in the Indianapolis 500, with Ford-powered cars taking the top four positions.
- 1966—Driving a Ford GT40 Mark II, Bruce McLaren and Chris Amon lead a 1-2-3 finish to win 24 Hours of Le Mans.
- 1967—Dan Gurney and A. J. Foyt codrive a GT40 MK IV to victory at Le Mans while Mario Andretti wins the Daytona 500 in a Fairlane.
- 1968—Ford wins its eighth NASCAR Manufacturers' Championship, and David Pearson wins the driver's title in his Torino.
- 1969—David Pearson wins his second NASCAR Winston Cup championship, driving a Holman-Moody Ford Torino Talladega.
- 1969—Ford wins its ninth NASCAR Manufacturers' Championship while Lee Roy Yarbrough takes the Daytona 500 in his Ford Talladega.

had confided in fellow racers that maybe it was time for him to hang up the driving suit. He had raced full time since he was 19 and at 34 had won all the major races. It seemed that burnout might have set in.

On Memorial Day at Charlotte, Lorenzen decided to take it easy in the World 600. He and team manager Herb Nab figured it was a long race and they should try to stay out of the

craziness during the opening laps. Lorenzen started on the pole, but about five laps into the event Nab told Lorenzen to back out of it when Fireball and the others started banging fenders for the lead. As Lorenzen came around turn two on to the backstretch he saw a car on fire. "That's when I saw the wreck on the backstretch. That's when he [Roberts] got upside down and burned. When he died five weeks later, it sort

Fearless Freddy Lorenzen was Ford's golden boy driver, winning at all the major super speedways. (Photo: Ford Motor Company)

The famed Holman-Moody team kept Ford in the limelight during the 1960s with precision race cars and top driving talent. (Photo: Ford Motor Company)

of took the big spark out of me." Lorenzen confessed he was tired of the continual grind of the racing life, and when Roberts died, it put him on course for retirement.

Lorenzen went on to win races through 1967 but just didn't have his heart in it anymore. After a brilliant but short career, Lorenzen decided to leave NASCAR after the 1967 season. "You've won everything and you get so tired of traveling—you're never home. I liked to water ski and finally quit."

Lorenzen tried reentering NASCAR in the 1970s but never quite made it work. "You lose all your team, and it takes a long time to put all that together again."

When asked if he ever regretted quitting at such a young age Lorenzen replied, "Maybe 4,000,000 percent. I was the stupidest guy, but the fun and glory weren't there anymore. I wish I had never quit."

Along with his dashing good looks, Lorenzen brought to NASCAR driving talent and business savvy not seen before. In 1964 he won 8 of the 16 races he entered and had 26 total NASCAR career wins. In 1963 Lorenzen became the first driver to win more than $100,000 in one season.

In the 1960s Fords came on strong in NASCAR, winning 23 events in 1963, 30 races in 1964 and an amazing 48 firsts in 1965. Ford's win record from 1960 to '69 overshadowed all other manufacturers with 145 wins. Plymouth was second, thanks to Richard Petty with 122 wins, and Dodge and Chevrolet followed at 67 and 53 wins respectively.

Dual Exhausts and Daytona

By 1968 Ford was back on top of its stock car game, running neck-and-neck with the Hemi-powered Plymouths. Ford had 20 victories

to Plymouth's 16. They realized that the Dodge Chargers and Plymouth Superbirds would give them trouble in 1969 with their wind-cutting aerodynamics, so Ford brought the Torino Talladega out for the challenge.

Aerodynamics was very much a top priority in 1969, although most of the NASCAR teams were still doing a lot of experimenting in every area to find an edge. This was especially important for Ford products because NASCAR ruled that the new 429 semi-Hemi had not been installed in 500 or more production Fords and would not be eligible for the event. To the relief of NASCAR, Ford Motor Company decided to come to the party anyway, bringing their new Talladegas with the wedge 427 V-8, the Ford power from the previous season.

Everyone expected the Fords to get blown away by the Dodge Chargers and Plymouth

Superbirds, but that notion was quickly dispelled when David Pearson set a new track record of more than 190 mph in his Wood Brothers Mercury Cyclone, a spin-off of the Talladega.

Junior Johnson had hung up his driving helmet and was now a team owner, campaigning a 427 V-8 powered Ford Talladega with Lee Roy Yarbrough at the wheel. "We went to Daytona to do some testing and was looking for anything that would help the car," said Johnson in his slow, deep drawl. "We took the exhausts and ran them out the back of the car." Though not against NASCAR rules, all entries traditionally ran exhaust pipes out either side of the car, just ahead of the rear wheels. "It did something to the air on the back of the car," said Johnson of the rerouting. "It streamlined the thing, it drove a lot better and it run a lot better in a straight line, helping the car with another three to four miles per hour."

During practice for the February Daytona 500, Junior's team ran the exhausts out the side, not wanting to raise any suspicions with the other teams. "On race morning we laid them up underneath the car again." According to Johnson, "There was no rule against it or nothin'."

Once the race was under way Dodge Charger pilot Buddy Baker moved within inches of Yarbrough to start slipstreaming down the backstretch. "Those two exhausts pipes was sittin' right in his radiator," chuckled Johnson, "and he'd stay there just a little bit and then drop way back and we played with 'em all day long." Baker's engine temperature would shoot up to the red mark each time Yarbrough's rear-mounted exhausts fried the Charger's front grille. No one could draft Yarbrough. By the closing laps of the race, Yarbrough started his move to the front, drafting past the other racers in his Talladega "heat machine." For the last 20

Fireball Roberts (#22) drives under Junior Johnson's Chevrolet (#3) followed by Dan Gurney (#0) in the 1963 Daytona 500. (Photo: Ford Motor Company)

Bill Stroppe's team carried the Mercury banner during the mid-1960s. Stroppe had numerous drivers including Darel Dieringer and Parnelli Jones. (Photos: The Bill Stroppe Collection)

Fireball Roberts drove his purple Holman-Moody Ford to victory in the 1963 Daytona Firecracker event in July. During his career, Roberts had also driven Chevrolets, Oldsmobiles and Pontiacs. (Photo: Ford Motor Company)

Dan Gurney drove everything from Formula One to stock cars. Ford used this cartoon-style series to promote its Total Performance program.

laps he was chasing down Charlie Glotzbach's Dodge Charger, running on softer tires to get more grip in the corners. He closed the gap on Glotzbach until the Talladega was set for a last-lap pass. As they came out of the fourth and final turn, Lee Roy slipped smoothly out of the draft and by the Dodge on the outside, stunning Chrysler executives, who had expected their products to dominate the 500-mile classic. Lee Roy and his trusty Talladega crossed the finish line with the Dodge glued to his rear bumper and Glotzbach's temperature gauge still rising.

Junior Johnson loved the Talladega, even before being allowed to use the new 429 V-8. "That was a nice machine for sure. You won't never see any more of them with the exhaust pipes sittin' out the back." NASCAR changed the rules shortly after the race, specifying that all exhausts would now exit to the side just in front of the rear wheels.

Legends of Riverside

Leonard Wood once said, "I want to tell you who's got some talent and that's Dan Gurney." In 1963 Leonard and Glen Wood, better known as the Wood Brothers, went to Riverside and found that Ford had assigned Dan Gurney to the Holman-Moody car and moved Fred Lorenzen to the Wood Brothers' car. "So we go to Riverside in '63 and Dan Gurney is in Holman-Moody's car just flyin'. He's very impressive. I remember watching him come through turn nine, watching him come off the corner and shifting gears." They knew Gurney was the man to get the job done. "But we didn't have too good a luck with Lorenzen. He got it upside down and off the track during the race," said Leonard. Gurney laughed as he remembered the incident. "He was trying to get through turn one really, really fast and just didn't make it!" Gurney won the race.

By January the Wood Brothers had Gurney in their car for the 1964 Riverside 500. Gurney won the Riverside 500 five times in six years from 1963 to '68. Four of those were with the Wood Brothers' team. Gurney described their professionalism and attention to detail as second to none. "I would say they were

at the beginning of their prime. They were clearly the best team from my perspective. They had uncovered a way to do pit stops better than any other team at that time. The Wood Brothers were just terrific. Life is full of luck, but to be a part of that team once or twice a year I almost felt embarrassed," said Gurney about his good fortune.

Sometimes winning too much can be a problem. Gurney knew that the heads of NASCAR were not too happy about one team, one brand and one driver, especially a California driver, winning all the events at Riverside. For many years the secret to NASCAR's success had been assuring variety in winning cars and drivers. After Gurney's fourth win in a row, he started to feel the pressure.

"In the end NASCAR kind of arranged it so I wasn't there with the Wood Brothers anymore," said Gurney. But he still has great respect for several NASCAR drivers and makes no bones about who they are. He admires the talents of Junior Johnson, Curtis Turner and especially David Pearson. Having had the chance to go up against many of the sixties'

NASCAR legends he said one driver stood out. "I knew Fireball [Roberts] very well. We were going to share a car at Le Mans before he died. I was not racing with him, but we were talking seriously about it. Fireball was a charismatic kind of an athlete who could have an intimidating presence. I think the guy had enormous talent—he just oozed talent. He was pretty sensational."

Monte Carlo Rally and the Falcon

Ford wanted to increase its reputation as an automotive giant worldwide, and racing was one way to generate the publicity. The company chose to support the Formula One racing engines that became the dominant power plant during the 1960s. Ford also participated in European rally racing and the Manufacturers' Championship series. Henry II wanted Ford to be known as an American car company that could compete with Europe's finest.

One of Ford's early successes came from entering three factory Falcon Sprints in the Monte Carlo Rally in 1963. This was primarily an effort to raise Falcon's profile, increase international press for Ford and, they hoped, advertise a positive Falcon performance. As the first American manufacturer to enter the rally, Ford hired Swedish driving ace Bo Ljungfeldt, Peter Jopp and pilot Anne Hall.

Shortly after the event got under way, the three cars got caught in an ice storm. Hall decided to take another route and ultimately was disqualified for her late arrival at the next checkpoint. Ljungfeldt and Jopp finally got through the line of stuck rally vehicles and headed on, with the Ljungfeldt car having numerous difficulties including a bad water hose, a clutch repair and a blowout while traveling more than 100 mph. While he put on a valiant drive,

At the 1964 Riverside 500, Roberts wasn't bashful about pushing his Holman-Moody Ford into the lead. Dan Gurney praised his raw talent.

Ned Jarrett won a total of 50 races driving both Fords and Chevrolets. He won both of his championships in Fords.

Fred Lorenzen (#28) and Parnelli Jones (#15) enjoyed bumper-to-bumper racing at Daytona.

Fred Lorenzen (left) and Dick Hutcherson (right) both drove for Holman-Moody during the mid-1960s. The Holman-Moody team is considered one of the most successful stock car racing teams of all time. (Photos this page: Ford Motor Company)

David Pearson had tremendous success with Ford in his blue-and-gold Holman-Moody Torino during the late 1960s, winning the NASCAR Driver's Championship in 1968 and 1969.

David Pearson was highlighted in Ford advertising for his amazing victory record.

Ljungfeldt could not make up the lost time, and the best chance of a high finish was in Jopp's hands.

The final leg from Chambery to Monaco included six high-speed runs favoring the powerful V-8 Falcons. This allowed both Ljungfeldt and Jopp to make up time, and Bo posted overall best times in all six of the stages. Jopp finished 35th overall and Ljungfeldt, 43rd. This placed them first and second in their class and gave Ford the opportunity to publish its own employee newspaper headline reading, "Falcon Sprint—Victor in Monte Carlo Rally." The V-8 engines in the Falcons required that they pay a heavy time handicap penalty, giving great advantage to the overall winner, Erik Carlsson, in his small-displacement Saab. With the Falcons winning their class, though, Ford had all the ammunition they needed. They started an advertising campaign that would suggest an overall win at Monte Carlo and promote the new Falcon Sprint to the American public. Mission accomplished.

Cobras, Sidewalks and France

While Carroll Shelby and his Cobras played a major role in Ford racing history and won the Manufacturers' Championship in 1965, the essence of driving a Cobra in competition was often missed in written records. Most stories written about the amazing Cobra do not capture the thunder of the open headers, the exhaust fumes in the cockpit or the adrenaline the drivers felt hauling down a narrow French highway at harrowing speeds. Some of the best Cobra stories are from races not won.

By the early 1960s Ford Motor Company under Henry II's direction was back into racing after a few years' absence. In the States, Ford was dominating Daytona and readying engines for Indianapolis. But the company wanted to be known as a world player in competition and, after Ferrari rebuffed a purchase offer, Henry chose to go it alone and spent plenty of cash getting to the top.

One of Ford's most prudent decisions was to support former Le Mans champion Carroll Shelby. Shelby's Ford-powered Cobra roadsters were trouncing Corvette, Ferrari and Porsche in the States. He had drivers like Bob Bondurant, Dan Gurney, Ken Miles and Phil Hill as pilots and was itching to take on Europe. Ford wanted the international recognition and teamed up with Shelby to go after the GT Class Manufacturers' Championship.

The Ford GT program was warming up, but it would be two more years before they would dominate Le Mans. Shelby's Cobras gave Ford quick victories over Ferrari, including a GT Class win in the 1964 24 Hours of Le Mans with Bondurant and Gurney driving a Daytona Coupe. Cobras were winning key events in 1964 and would win the Manufacturers' Championship in 1965 with Bondurant at the wheel. According to Bondurant, who savored each day he raced in Europe, one of his favorite events was the Tour de France.

"It was wonderful. Between each race and hill climb you're doing a rally. After any event, the car is always in impound and unavailable for any mechanical work until the next race segment starts." The 1964 event challenged the resources of Bondurant and co-driver Jochen Neerpasch as they drove the Daytona Coupe CSX2300 to its limits.

Early in the event they realized the car was taking on carbon monoxide in the cockpit from a broken exhaust system, so they picked up a small, flat piece of wood. "I would have Jochen stick the piece of wood out the window to bring some fresh air in and I would open my door to draft the carbon monoxide out." Most of this was happening above 140 mph.

Next Bondurant had to "fix" a broken throttle cable by placing a French franc under the linkage, setting the Cobra in full-throttle position. "I put it in gear, fired it up and drove by shutting the ignition off going in to the corners. You had to be prepared to hang on when you turned the throttle back on!" They had the pit crew change it during the next stage.

"So now we're late and the other cars have already left. Coming down the highway I said, 'We need fuel.' I told Jochen to grab one side and I would grab the other." The Daytona Coupe had quick-fill tanks on either side. "So we were filling it up and a little Frenchman came out to admire the car. When we got done we threw the hoses back to him, jumped in the car and took off! He must have been saying. 'Gosh those crazy Americans stole my gas!' So we got down the road to our emergency pit stop and said, 'You'd better take care of that guy back at the station.' "

The crew topped off the gas tanks and, according to Bondurant, "That's when we really hauled ass as we came to the city of Rouen." They drove directly into a traffic jam and knew they somehow had to get through it or be late for the next stage, which would mean disqualification. "We were blinking the lights and honking the horn and finally got to an intersection where we had to drive up on the sidewalk." He jumped the curb and started making time down the sidewalk, honking the horn and sounding off the open headers as people dove clear of the Coupe. When they made it through the intersection they pulled the Cobra back on to the street with more than a few people shaking their fists. They headed south.

Ferrari 250 GTOs swept the 1964 Daytona 2000 Kilometer event with Cobra pilot Dan Gurney taking fourth overall. Dave MacDonald in the #14 Daytona Coupe slips by Jef Stevens' roadster. MacDonald went out with differential problems and a spectacular pit fire while Stevens' roadster retired around the same time with a fuel leak.

Gurney pits for fuel and oil as the sun sets over Daytona. (Photos this page: Ford Motor Company)

The start of the 1966 24 hours of Le Mans event saw a host of Ford GT Mark IIs—the "Ford Armada" as Enzo Ferrari described it. (Photo: Ford Motor Company)

Their next destination would be the beach, and that meant driving for many miles down a narrow highway with no shoulder. "We were doing 150 or 160 mph down the road. When you came up on another car, you had to judge your distance because it was a two-lane highway. And beach traffic was coming back so you'd blast by [a car] and duck back in again." Bicycles, cars and old farmhouses were a blur as they charged toward the next stage. "We did that for 45 minutes to an hour and Jochen had never put on a seat belt—they didn't use seat belts much at that time. So I looked over and he was putting it on, and he said, 'Please, please be careful, Bob.' And I said, 'Don't worry. Self-preservation prevails!'"

"When we finally arrived at our checkpoint, we had 16 seconds to spare or we would have been disqualified." After a valiant run they later lost a clutch in the

Le Mans section of the event and had to drop out, taking a DNF after a nine-day adventure.

Bondurant and Dan Gurney teamed up to win the June Le Mans event in the GT category that year and could have won first overall except for a bad oil cooler that slowed them.

Driving a Cobra in 1965, Bondurant won every event he entered—and the GT Class Manufacturers' Championship for Shelby and Ford.

Le Mans, Fords and Henry II

Henry II went to Le Mans in June 1962 to watch the famed French road-racing event. It struck him that with Ferrari winning the event in 1958, 1960, 1961 and again in his presence in 1962, it would take a major manufacturer to upset that kind of dominance. It was ironic that in 1959, the year Ferrari did not win, they were aced by Carroll

Shelby driving an Aston Martin. Henry first considered the easy thing to do—buy Ferrari—but was rebuffed in the eleventh hour by founder Enzo. Henry II next decided to spend whatever it took to build a new race car and team from scratch and make his mark on France.

After Ford engineers and race program managers brainstormed many ideas, they decided the new race car would need to have a top speed of around 200 mph and average close to 120 mph for the event. The new design was rushed through prototyping and early testing and experienced many failures before the engineers worked out the design flaws to be expected in any new program.

After many millions of dollars and numerous starts, the Ford GT program was still finding the Ferrari team a very tough challenge. At Le Mans in 1964 the two Ford entries were sidelined with gearbox problems, and in

1965 the Ford GTs again failed to finish, although they did set a one-lap speed record of 141 mph. Fortunately, the team did take the first three positions at the Daytona 2,000 kilometer endurance event in 1965, making both Ford and Shelby confident that they had a capable team.

Going in to Le Mans in 1966, the Ford team was under the direction of Shelby for the second year. Ken Miles had already won the Daytona 24-hour endurance event and Sebring for Ford, and it was obvious that their speed and reliability were where they needed to be. The team was well prepared in every respect for Le Mans. The drivers were the best the world had to offer, the cars were reliable 427 V-8 powered monsters and the team was operating like a well-oiled machine.

Henry II was at the big event to watch as his Fords dominated. Enzo Ferrari referred to the Ford team as the "steamroller," and by four o'clock the next afternoon Ford had finally topped Ferrari in speed, smoothness and durability. Only 15 vehicles were still running in the event when the checkers fell.

During the final lap Henry Ford II, special vehicle director Leo Beebe and Carroll Shelby made a joint decision to have the three lead cars come across the finish line together for a press photo opportunity that would be seen around the world. Bruce McLaren and Chris Amon had been running in second place in their black number two car and stayed just behind the number one car of Ken Miles and Denny Hulme. Unfortunately, Le Mans officials noted that because the number two car had started approximately 30 yards behind the Miles/Hulme car, it had traveled farther and therefore was the winner—a result Ford did not intend. Miles left his race car standing and skipped the traditional owner's champagne

Ford's J-Car program was being developed for the 1967 season. It was the test bed for the Le Mans–winning Mark IV.

Carroll Shelby's slow Texas drawl belied his racing genius. His Ford GT racers consistently outpaced the Holman-Moody team cars. (Photos this page: Ford Motor Company)

toast with Henry II and his wife, heading instead for the seclusion of his hotel. One published report said he had planned to retire from racing "after winning Le Mans."

"Henry Ford, Leo Beebe and I screwed up," said Shelby. "We decided to have them come across the finish line together and they [Le Mans officials] made up a rule. The one that started farthest back had traveled farther. I've always been ashamed of that because if anybody ever deserved that [win] it was Ken Miles," said Shelby.

Lead driver Ken Miles was set to run again but died in a tragic

accident while testing the Ford J-Car at Riverside in August 1966.

Nineteen sixty-seven would be Ford Motor Company's last stand at Le Mans as a factory effort. Under team leader Carroll Shelby, Ford was again ready for the challenge, bringing four new Mark IV models, three Mark IIs and a Mark I to the event. The Mark IV team drivers were Foyt-Gurney; McLaren-Donahue, Bianchi-Andretti and Hulme-Ruby.

The red number one Mark IV had a "bubble" in the roof over the driver to accommodate Gurney's tall frame and helmet. This also caused teammate Foyt some

Both Foyt and Gurney liked the Mark IV. "I guess they thought we were abusing it because we were outrunning all the others real bad—the other Fords, Chaparrals and the Ferraris," said Foyt.

Ford's racing investment in the GT program had already paid off in 1966 at Le Mans. The 1967 event was icing on the cake with Henry II's all-American car and team winning the event over Ferrari.

A. J. Foyt and Dan Gurney were at the wheel for an all-American victory at Le Mans in 1967. "It was plenty fast—faster than the Ferraris we had to run against," said Gurney of the red Mark IV. "We had 5 mph on them." (Photos this page: Ford Motor Company)

problems as he had to stretch for the steering wheel, being shorter in stature. "I kind of got shafted in that car," said Foyt, laughing. "Around four o'clock in the morning I pulled in and got out and they told me I had to get back in. I said 'What do you mean I got to get back in? My shoulders are sore!' They said, 'We can't find Gurney.' I said, 'We got relief drivers,' and they said, 'No, you guys are doin' too good.' So I got back in it and I told Gurney, 'I'm goin' to get even with you some day.'" He and Gurney still laugh about it.

Foyt knew winning Le Mans would require a combination of hard driving and yet keeping the car together. "We ran it pretty hard but still not where we were abusing it. I guess they thought we were abusing it because we were outrunning all the others real bad—the other Fords, Chaparrals and the Ferraris." All Ford drivers, including Foyt, knew the ultimate goal of the event. "The Ferraris, that's what Henry Ford wanted us to beat."

While top speed down the Mulsanne Straight was critical to winning, it could also be harrowing. "We were running right at 220 mph. The only bad thing was the little Renaults were running about 140 mph and they would be drafting. At night you would catch some of them and it would give you a really big thrill." The painted trees close to the edge of the straight were also disconcerting to Foyt. "They used to whitewash them trees and I wish to hell they wouldn't." He said it was almost better not to see how close the trees were to the track's edge. His bright driving lights were strobing across the trees as he flew down the long straight. "I kept saying, 'If I make a mistake I'm goin' out amongst them babies.' I'd just as soon have them dark where you didn't see them."

Gurney loved the Ford Mark IV. "I thought it was an extraordinarily comfortable car, really. We sort of fine-tuned it in terms of front and rear ride heights and rear spoiler heights. We got that [done] and the thing was darn near perfect. It was a very comfortable car to drive. I don't think it would run more than about 215 mph. It was plenty fast—faster than the Ferraris we had to run against. We had 5 mph on them."

Gurney knew that approaching Le Mans as an all-out speed event would not win the race. "I really never did give a full, hard lap. The Achilles heel of that car was probably the fact that it weighed 3,200 pounds and the brakes couldn't stop it very many times. Other than that, it was bulletproof and easy to drive. It was more like a passenger car than a race car."

Gurney and Foyt became American heroes overnight after the international win at Le Mans. "Certainly when you have won a very prestigious race you are smitten," said Gurney. "While it wasn't a classic approach to getting the job done, it certainly got the job done. And in fact we not only won the race but also the index of performance, which had to do with fuel mileage and things like that. So it really rattled the Europeans' cages."

Indy— Changing of the Dynasty

Indianapolis had been dominated by the Offenhauser four-cylinder engine for 18 straight years. From 1947 to '64 front-engined roadsters had used the amazing power plant to record victories under driving greats such as Mauri Rose, Bill Vukovich, Sam Hanks, Roger Ward, Jim Rathmann, Parnelli Jones and eventual four-time winner A. J. Foyt. All that started to change

when a talented 31-year-old grand prix driver decided he wanted to tackle the Indianapolis brickyard.

"I realized that it was such a dominant institution," said Californian Dan Gurney. "In those days there wasn't another race, even globally, outside of the Le Mans 24-hour race, that had the history and prestige that the Indianapolis 500 had. I think that if you were a racing driver you felt compelled to participate."

Since starting in his first Formula One event in 1959, Gurney had seen a revolution in racing design. "Since I was experienced in grand prix racing in Europe, I witnessed the end of the front-engined grand prix era and a coming of the rear-engine era. It essentially made the front-engined cars obsolete in Europe. Obviously once you saw that demonstrated, there was no doubt it was only a matter of time before the same thing would happen at Indy."

Gurney decided he would try to make the field at Indy in 1962. "I felt well, golly, why not try to be a part of that inevitable revolution?" Gurney hoped to do more than race in the event. He wanted to use it as a springboard to bring a whole new team to Indy in 1963. "At that point in time a guy named Colin Chapman was the head of Lotus, and he was adventuresome as well. So I said, 'Colin, may I invite you to come to the speedway in 1962 to watch the race?' with the idea of possibly getting together with someone like Ford Motor Company. He right away said, 'Yes, I'll do it.' So I bought his round-trip ticket to come see the '62 race, which happened to be my first 500 and my first oval race."

Colin Chapman observed the event and the sprinkling of rear-engined cars, and apparently saw Indy as an opportunity. "I introduced him to the people at Ford," said Gurney, "and out of this Jimmy [Clark] and I became teammates in what was a Lotus-Ford attempt at Indy.

Indy 500 winner Jimmy Clark was one of the world's best drivers. According to Dan Gurney, "He would jump in almost anything and give it a whale of a ride." (Photo: Ford Motor Company)

That was a real adventure. It got Ford's interest, and in the end it was the source of a good deal of the money and it was an opening for what became a good, successful Ford."

Jimmy Clark was already driving for Colin Chapman and Lotus, so the idea of a talented two-man team driving Lotus cars with Ford engines at Indy seemed like a good idea. "Chapman didn't think it was going to require more than about 350–60 horsepower. The rest of the competitiveness was going to come out of the chassis."

"In 1963 they were on Firestone tires, smaller diameter tires than the rest of the field." The weak point of the 1963 cars, according to Gurney, was reliability. "I think I started the race on about seven cylinders. I wasn't real pleased about that."

Clark finished second that year, trailing Jones, who used all his skill and experience for the win, but not without controversy. Jones' Offy-powered roadster developed an oil leak late in the race and Clark, in second, was sure the Offy would either be black-flagged or drop out of the event. But Jones continued to command the lead and pulled off his first and only victory at Indy. According to the smiling Gurney, "That's why we called him Parn-oily!"

The 1964 Indy 500 classic was another frustrating year for the Lotus-Ford team. Having been told they would race on Dunlop tires, Clark and Gurney had no choice but to deal with the disadvantage. All other cars were using Firestones, well proven to be faster and more durable. Gurney noted, "They [Dunlops] just weren't up to the task and started to come apart." With many extra pit stops for new rubber, Gurney was hopelessly out of contention.

A. J. Foyt finished first, but it would be the last time a roadster chassis would see the winner's circle. Roger Ward finished second in his rear-engined Watson-Ford while Gurney lost a tire tread and settled for 17th position. Clark had a suspension failure and finished 24th. The Ford cammer engines performed flawlessly, promising one less thing to worry about for the next Indy.

Gurney described Foyt as a person and a driver. "He was certainly the young superstar and full of himself, but also extraordinarily bright about his approach to it all. He was very, very good and I really didn't get to know him much until we shared a car at Le Mans." The talented Foyt wasn't shy about his own talents as a driver. "His bragging didn't bother me in the least," said Gurney. "He could back it up. Even though he was known for being able to intimidate his rivals, he was a very fair driver. He didn't knock people off the track. You could run wheel to wheel with him."

The Wood Brothers were asked by Ford to try their hand at pitting for Jimmy Clark in the 1965 race and they agreed. The Wood Brothers arrived at the track early to study, prepare and make any necessary changes in the pit process for Clark's Lotus-Ford. "We went up a week early and walked into the garage, and had they resented us being there we would have probably never done it. But they seemed to welcome us in and turned that part of it over to us to do as we saw fit." The Wood Brothers started preparations for making faster tire changes and streamlining the refueling system. Having made a number of changes that were quite different from what Indy race teams were used to, they then had to get their system through track inspection.

When the USAC inspector came around to their pit position, he wanted to know why they chose to set up their fuel tank the way they did. "He said he would bet $1,000 that we couldn't pour 20 gallons a minute out of that thing. We didn't really care what he thought as long as he passed us on the inspection." When it came time to practice fueling the car, they pumped a full 58 gallons in 15 seconds.

Jimmy Clark's year at Indy was 1965, as he effectively led from start to finish in his Ford-powered Lotus 38. Parnelli Jones finished second, also driving a Lotus-Ford. The top four finishers were rear-engined Fords, and the roadster days were effectively over. Clark was the first non-American to win Indy since Italy's Dario Resta won in 1916 driving a Peugeot, and he was also the first winner to average more than 150 mph for the race.

Gurney admired Clark, arguably one of the best Formula One drivers of all time. "Jimmy loved racing, he raced for his Scottish heritage and was very, very talented. He had a lot of

Dan Gurney (#91) and Jimmy Clark (#92) showed great potential in their initial 1963 Indianapolis 500. Gurney eventually dropped out of the event while Clark finished second to Parnelli Jones' roadster.

Jimmy Clark drove his #6 Lotus Ford at Indy in 1964, making it clear that the roadsters' days were numbered.

In 1965 Jimmy Clark and car owner–builder Colin Chapman dominated the Indy 500, relegating the front-engined racers to museums. (Photos this page: Ford Motor Company)

Clark's crew gives his #92 a last-minute checkover before sending the Scot out for a practice lap for the 1963 Indianapolis 500.

Jimmy Clark (right) and Jackie Stewart talk race strategies before the start of the 1967 Indy event. (Photos this page: Ford Motor Company)

confidence in his driving abilities. He would jump in almost anything and give it a whale of a ride," said Gurney. "His fans admired that a great deal. He was basically a great guy—pretty quiet but he had a mischievous streak in him. Good sense of humor."

Asked if he thought the British learned anything special from competing at Indy, Gurney said,

"Well, that's an interesting thing. By the time the Euros and Brits get through writing history, it'll look like the Americans didn't know anything. Their tires failed when they first ran here; their wheels collapsed." Gurney said that chassis tuning and tire technology were things the Americans were more advanced in. "As a matter of fact, Lotus learned a whale of

a lot about racing, even though they called these American cars dinosaurs—they learned a lot from these dinosaur people."

Thunderbolts Strike

In 1963 Chrysler vehicles were dominating drag racing, and both Ford and General Motors were hustling to get back in the hunt. Because Chrysler had the Hemi coming out the next year, Ford needed to shed the 427 Galaxie lightweight, apparently not light enough, and come up with something substantially faster. The Ford Special Vehicles group went to work stuffing a 427 high-rise V-8 into a mid-size Fairlane 500 chassis. All development was done at Ford's Dearborn Proving Ground under Vern Tinsler and Charlie Grey. The 1963 Peacock Blue prototype was then shipped to Tasca Ford for review and then to Dearborn Steel Tubing (DST) to produce 100 of the ultra-fast Fairlanes. DST specialized in producing limited runs of high-performance cars for Ford.

"I did the development driving before they actually turned the contract over to DST for production," said Len Richter, then a 32-year-old Ford test driver. "Ford developed it through Charlie Grey in the Special Vehicles group. My job, day in and day out, was running Thunderbolts on the straightaway [at the proving ground track]." Richter had his dream job with Ford: "Ford was paying me to do this! They would send me around the country, paying for my hotel and airfare and still give me a paycheck." His car was sponsored by the Bob Ford dealership, now Fairlane Ford, in Dearborn, Michigan.

Driving at the Dearborn Proving Ground facility allowed Richter to have a full-length drag strip at his disposal for testing and the Ford X-Garage on-site to do all the mechanical work. "We were trying transmissions, axle shafts, gear combinations and carburetor setups."

The Thunderbolts were turning quarter mile speeds of 128 to 130 mph through the traps. "At the Winternationals it got down to Tasca Ford and me for the Stock Eliminator trophy run, and just previous to that I broke an axle shaft. Due to the live television coverage, they didn't allow me time to change the shaft so Tasca Ford had to make the run on its own for the championship. And at that time I had them covered on both elapsed time and speed, so it would have been a very good race," said Richter. Richter drove for Bob Ford through 1966, driving lightweight Galaxies, Thunderbolts and an AF/X Mustang with a single overhead cam 427 V-8.

When the Thunderbolts hit the drag racing circuit, they were an instant success. All Thunderbolts were equipped with dual four-barrel carburetors and were factory rated at 425 horsepower. Thunderbolt aficionado Dennis Kolodziej points out that the engines likely produced well more than 500 horsepower and most were further modified by the individual teams. "The amazing fact was that out of 100 Thunderbolts built, just over half were equipped with Lincoln automatic transmissions. They didn't perform or hold up very well and most were quickly converted to four-speed manuals."

Technically street legal, the Thunderbolts carried fiberglass front fenders, front bumpers and hoods. The doors on factory-sponsored models were also fiberglass. The front bumper was later made of aluminum due to a National Hot Rod Association (NHRA) rules change. The first 11 Thunderbolts had Plexiglas side and rear windows, and some used the lightweight material for the windshield as well. Once chief engineer Tinsler found that the

The Thunderbolt engines were all Ford 427 models with dual four-barrel carburetors rated conservatively at 425 horsepower. The front fenders, bumpers and hoods were all fiberglass to keep the weight down.

Gas Ronda is still considered a legend in drag racing and won two Plymouth Barracudas by winning major events in his Thunderbolt.

Out of 100 Thunderbolts built, slightly more than half were shipped with automatic transmissions that did not survive well under the pressures of drag racing. Most were converted to four-speed transmissions. (Photos this page: Gas Ronda collection)

car wouldn't make the minimum weight of 3,205 pounds, he went back to the glass rear window for the rest of the run. "The interiors were stripped of all sound deadening, carpeting, heaters and radios," said Kolodziej. "But they did have front and rear seats to qualify for the Super Stock category they competed in."

Never meant to mate with a Fairlane, the 427 V-8 installation was difficult at best. The shock towers, control arms and suspension all had to be heavily modified to accommodate the 500 horsepower cast iron block.

After the first two cars were produced, several top drivers were invited to Dearborn to pick up their Thunderbolts. Among that group was top drag racer Gaspar Ronda, better known as "Gas."

Gas Ronda was immediately intrigued. "It was fantastic. We had been running against the lighter Chryslers, and this was the first time we had a car where we were on even or better footing with the competition," said Ronda. "We were very excited about it." He said the Thunderbolt could launch off the line with just about any competitor, even though the automatics in the Chryslers were expected to provide the Hemis with an advantage. "It was great to pull up alongside an automatic and pull ahead every time you hit another gear. They just couldn't believe I could jump ahead of them each time I shifted."

NHRA rules for the Super Stock class required vehicles to use rear tires no wider than seven inches. With so much power, the Thunderbolts were at their best with bigger rubber on the ground. "We were in a way handicapped in NHRA when we ran on the narrow tires," said Ronda. The American Hot Rod Association (AHRA) allowed drag slick tires in their events, helping the Thunderbolts put even more power to the ground.

"There was a knack to launching the Thunderbolt," said Ronda. "I was very fortunate in getting a feel for how to do it and, consequently, won the Super Stock title. It was one of the most fun cars I ever drove, and I wish I still had my Thunderbolt today."

An NHRA article described Ronda's championship run: "Top Stock Eliminator winner Gas Ronda actually scored a double victory. Not only did he repeatedly meet and defeat the best drivers in the nation in 'dragsters' of the Stock Car ranks—the big Super Stockers—he did it with a number two choice car among most of the contestants. Every time Ronda rolled into the pits there was a large and impressive field of Dodges and Plymouths, but in almost every case it was his famed orange colored '64 Ford Thunderbolt that was still around when the prizes and awards were handed out."

Gas Ronda is still considered a legend in drag racing and won two Plymouth Barracudas by winning major events in his Thunderbolts. He promptly put them on display at sponsor Russ Davis' Ford dealership with a sign that said, "I won them with a Ford." Ronda won the 1964 world points championship and held records in most of the NHRA divisions that year.

Top Thunderbolt drivers included Gas Ronda, Mickey Thompson, Les Richie, Len Richter, Don Turner, Phil Bonner, Bill Lawton, Clester Andrews and Paul Harvey. A total of 100 Thunderbolts (all based on Fairlane 500 hardtops) were built, including 59 automatics and 41 with four-speed manuals. DST also produced 21 A/FX Mercury Comet Cyclones and one Comet wagon, all with high-rise 427 V-8 engines.

Mustangs with Grit— Trans Am '67

In 1967 Ford Motor Company was sponsoring the Mercury team, led by Bud Moore, in Trans Am racing. Moore had a good budget and a dream team of drivers that included Parnelli Jones, Dan Gurney, David Pearson and Peter Revson. The lead Mustang team, however, was under Carroll Shelby's wing, working on a shoestring budget with a two-car team hauled around in trailers by fifth-wheel pickups.

According to 1987 SCCA GT Champion Rick Titus, son of the late Jerry Titus, the Shelby team was very thinly funded. "That's what made the accomplishment all that more spectacular," said Titus. "It is also what made it accomplishable. Because Ford didn't have a bunch of money in it, Ford didn't meddle in it. It wasn't until 1968 when Ford put some money into the effort and wanted to bring on the tunnel port [V-8] that they got overly involved." With Ford focusing on the Cougar team, there wasn't much assistance for Shelby in Trans Am.

Shelby went out on a limb by saying he wanted to put a relatively unknown *Sports Car Graphic* magazine editor Jerry Titus in his car. Ken Miles was actually the top name on the list, but he was busy with Ford GTs and Cobras. He had no time for what was then seen as an upstart series with little notoriety. "Because of Shelby's loyalty and confidence in my father," said Titus, "he put together a very small band of folks who built cars and no one really expected any results." The cars were not super cars, and the team realized by mid-season that Mark Donahue's Penske Camaro was making major gains in performance and race finishes. It would take a lot of dedicated driving by Jerry Titus for Mustang to repeat the title.

Dodge won the opening event at Daytona with Titus finishing fourth, just behind Parnelli Jones' Cougar. In the second event at Sebring, Titus was starting alongside Jones. He knew he would have his hands more than full trying to take the lead from Jones and also knew he needed to make his mark. About halfway around the course on the first lap Titus took the inside line, still side by side with Parnelli, going into a tight turn. Parnelli finally had nowhere to go but off the end and into a sand trap, leaving Titus in control of the lead and ultimately the win at Sebring.

Titus and team manager Lou Spencer both enjoyed toying with the competition's head, and at one event the Penske team became the focus. Titus had been dicing back and forth with Mark Donahue's Camaro for fastest qualifying time, and he felt he had a little more speed left in reserve. He told Spencer he thought he could go back out and nail down the fastest time of the day, but the manager told him to hold on a minute. Spencer first spray-painted a one-gallon fuel can flat black. Although it was filled with nothing more than legal racing fuel, Titus' crew made a point of thoroughly shaking the can in full view of the Penske team, as if mixing the substance. They then added the "mystery fuel" to the Mustang and began rocking the car from side to side just before Titus went back out on the track, setting the fastest time of the day. The Penske crew immediately filed a protest regarding the black can, almost certain the contents had improved Titus' performance. In the end, nothing but gas was found in the black can and Titus started from the pole.

Shelby's team had plenty of obstacles to overcome. Two new race cars were built and shipped out on a Ford transport for the 1967 Lime Rock race. The truck

Shelby's Mustang Trans Am team was a low-budget operation in 1967 compared to the other manufacturers. They had one backup car for top driver Jerry Titus and a second car that was used for various other Ford drivers.

The Ford five-liter V-8 produced plenty of power, and with little company involvement, the Shelby team managed to win the 1967 championship.

driver got off on the wrong road and tried sailing under an overpass that was too low, shearing both race cars off the top. With the new cars destroyed, two well-used race cars quickly had to be shipped out for the event. Titus still managed a third-place finish.

After 11 of the 12 events, Titus had all four Mustang wins under his belt, while Dodge had one victory, Cougar four and Camaro three. The final race at Pacific Raceway near Seattle would provide real racing drama. Cougar and Mustang were now within three points of each other and tied with four wins apiece. The Manufacturers' Championship lay in the outcome. A Mustang, any Mustang, needed to finish ahead of the Cougars to bring home the gold for Ford.

Regular rain showers kept the cars slipping and sliding throughout the weekend. During practice, Jerry Titus rolled his Mustang down a 400-foot embankment in a serious accident that left him cut, bruised and looking for a replacement car. According to Rick Titus, "They had no backup but went to John McComb who had a Shelby-built car and said, 'Look we've got to replace Jerry's car. Can we take yours?'" The answer was yes, and the Shelby crew went to work, staying up most of the night to get Titus' car ready for the event. "My father, though badly beat up, got back in that car and led, and then the motor popped." The blown engine would drop him to the back of the finish chart with only Ronnie Bucknum to carry the team colors. Driving the sister car, Bucknum finished second in a driving rain to Mark Donahue's Camaro, garnering enough points to give the championship to Ford.

The Cougar team also had their share of bad luck: A large rock smashed Gurney's windshield and teammate Jones became sick during the race while trying to manhandle his car around the course. Gurney finished third and gave Cougar a close second in the series championship.

Although the SCCA did not recognize a driver's championship during that period, the sanctioning body later admitted that not recognizing drivers was an oversight. The SCCA has now officially recognized champions for each year based on finishes, giving the driver's championship for 1967 to the late Jerry Titus. He's probably having a good laugh right now, still running at redline and nosing out the competition.

Hard-Charging Sixties

Ford racing in the 1960s was an era of fast cars, fortunes spent and dominance in nearly every area of the racing world. With drivers like Fireball Roberts, Dan Gurney, A. J. Foyt, Parnelli Jones, Jimmy Clark, Gas Ronda, Bob Bondurant and a host of others, all Ford had to do was provide top equipment and the trophies were theirs.

It was also a decade of losing great drivers like Fireball Roberts, Joe Weatherly, Jimmy Clark, Dave MacDonald, Eddie Sachs and others dying in competition, often with fire involved. Out of those tragedies came new safety rules, such as fuel cells, fire suits, window netting, full-face helmets and more stringent roll cage designs.

Track owners were also required to upgrade their facilities by installing concrete retaining walls in place of the old-style guardrails that regularly launched cars out of the park. They also added more fire and ambulance equipment and better on-site facilities for immediate medical attention. Ford Motor Company was a front runner in developing fast cars while supporting better safety features and rules for all the events.

The racers of the sixties had some rough edges, small paychecks and a life on the road, but they also enjoyed life-long friendships, hard racing and a good laugh. There was incredible talent in every area, and the world of racing may never see a magical period like it again.

The Fords of the sixties were nothing short of dominant in racing, and Ford will forever be indebted to the amazing drivers who brought them victory. The next time you visit Daytona, Le Mans or Riverside, give a salute to those young lions of racing.

Total Performance was Ford's theme through the mid-1960s, as Fords won in Indianapolis, NASCAR, Trans Am, Le Mans and sports car racing. (Photo: Ford Motor Company)